Embracing Womanhood

The Journey of a Queen

Dr. Cassundra White-Elliott

CLF Publishing, LLC.
9161 Sierra Ave, Ste. 203C
Fontana, CA 92335
www.clfpublishing.org

Cover Design by Senir Design. Contact information-info@senirdesign.com.

ISBN # 978-1-945102-15-8

Printed in the United States of America.

Acknowledgements

I acknowledge every person who reads this book or purchases it for someone to read. I pray that every hand the book passes through will be blessed.

If you are a believer in Christ and have committed your life to Him, you are a conduit through which His blessings can flow. Be a blessing to a young woman and help her to blossom as God intended from the time He created man. Show her she is worthy to be cherished and honored.

Dedications

This book is dedicated to all the precious flowers out there that God looks down on so lovingly.

Know that you are worthy of His love and His favor.

Believe in yourself and know that God created you in His image, and He wants you to stand tall and be counted.

You are not an outcast!

You are not a failure!

You are beautiful and uniquely designed by God!

Love who He has created you to be – even when others fail to see your worth!

God does not make mistakes, but we will make plenty. Just know, He will love you through them all!

Table of Contents

Introduction   7

Chapter One   11
Changes in My Body (Puberty)

Chapter Two   37
Knowing and Accepting Yourself (Self-Esteem)

Chapter Three   51
Setting Goals: Short and Long Term

Chapter Four   69
Finances

Chapter Five   95
Relationships

Chapter Six   105
Keeping a Healthy Mind (Mental Wellness)

Gift of Salvation   115

References   120

About the Author   121

Other Books by the Author   123

Introduction

As toddlers, children tend to be somewhat oblivious to the world around them, their impact on the world, and the world's impact on them. The older they get though, they begin to make connections between the world and themselves, as well as how they connect and relate to other people, such as their family, friends, and teachers. As children mature through toddlerhood and adolescence, if they are not properly trained in areas of important life aspects, they can go through life aloof and fail to be properly grounded. Without a solid foundation, these individuals may find themselves as adults underprepared for life, facing one ordeal or failure after another.

Read the following example to help understand the point I'm making. To have a successful business, one must be well-versed in the subject matter in which she is going into business. Example, if someone wants to be a successful landscaper by providing efficient service to her clients, he will need to know how to prune hedges, treat infected or diseased plants, cure fungi, etc. If as a landscaper he does not possess the necessary skills or infor-mation, the business will not thrive and will eventually fail. The same concept is true of life in general. To be successful in life, in the most basic sense, people should possess a healthy self-concept, know how to navigate through problems (problem-solving), be in tune with their body, be mentally stable, have a healthy attitude toward finances, relate well to others (relationships), and be skilled in setting goals.

Embracing Womanhood presents a survey of the afore-mentioned topics to assist teenagers and young women (ages 15 - 25), as they navigate from puberty to young adulthood, to become the women God preordained them to be. God said in I

Peter 2:9, *"But you are a chosen race, a royal priesthood, a holy nation..."* Therefore, women were designed to be queens, who are well equipped to reign in their specific areas of life. However, without guidance, they will fall prey to subservient attitudes and become victims of their circumstances.

Instance after instance and circumstance after circumstance in our society, captured and televised by the media, have demonstrated that the absence of guidance, modeling and information leads to a countless number of individuals falling into vicious cycles. The cycles include exponential failures, as individuals spin their wheels trying to figure out whether to go left or right at the fork in the road.

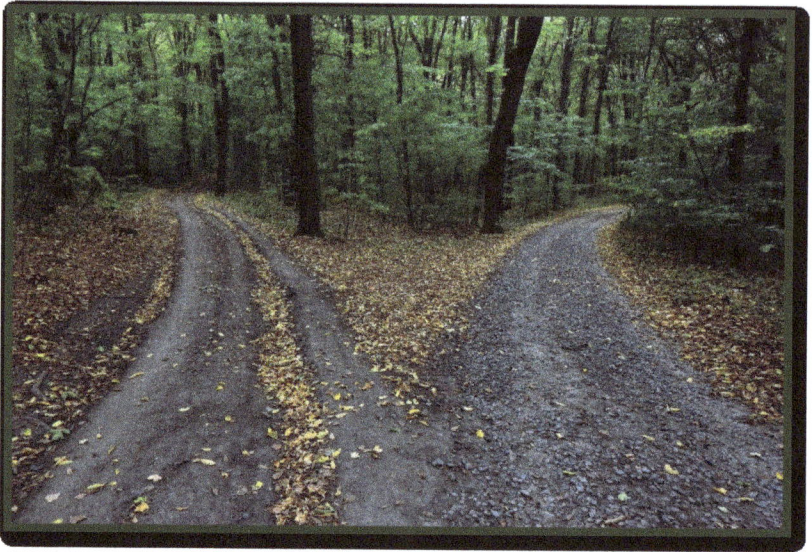

One unguided decision leads to another and another, and so on. To avoid many of the pitfalls of life, a solid foundation must be laid. Without a solid base on which to stand, people will fall time and time again.

Young ladies, it goes without saying that all people make mistakes at one time or another in their life. No one is perfect and without fault. So, I by no means propose this book will make you perfect or blameless, but it will give you a sense of security about making choices in and for your life that will be beneficial for you and those you come in contact with – if you utilize the guidance provided in each of the topics that will be surveyed within the pages of this book. **Dare to become the queen God already stated you are!**

Note – As you read, take notes in the margins and at the end of each section, to record your thoughts and identify questions you may have. If you should have more questions on a specific topic after reading the designated section, please use the list of references at the end of the book, do further research on your own, or speak to a trusted counselor/parent/guardian/pastor.

Chapter One

Changes in My Body
(Puberty)

Where Were You?

Where were you
When I started to grow
Where were you
When my puberty started to show

Where were you
When my mind was confused
Where were you
When I was being misused

Where were you
To teach me what I should know
Where were you
When I needed strength to grow

Mother,
Where were you?

by April Mitchell

Timing and Stages of Puberty

Adolescence and puberty can be very confusing! But, if you know what to expect during this time in your life, you may be able to handle the changes in your body and attitude better. Puberty is the stage between adolescence and adulthood. At times, you will feel like a child and at other times, you will feel as though you are being treated as a child and dislike the feeling. Just as you are trying to figure out the changes that are taking place in your body, your parents are trying to keep up and figure out the changes in your behavior and attitude.

Puberty in girls usually starts between the ages of 8 and 13 and ends around age 14. One of the first signs of puberty usually is a change in your breasts, as they start to grow. About two years later, you will begin to menstruate (have your period). In between, breast development and menstruation starting, you'll probably start to see more hair in places, such as under your arms and in your pubic area.

Puberty also involves big changes to your shape: a curvier shape, wider hips, thighs, and bottom, and normal weight gain as your body structure grows. Getting taller (which stops when puberty ends) is also a part of puberty. Be aware that you may have a growth spurt (where you get taller suddenly) and end up taller than some of the boys your age. Don't worry; they will catch up and eventually pass you.

Keep in mind that these changes all are common and normal! Also, make sure to take good care of your great, growing body. With everything that's going on, it is important to eat well, stay fit, and get enough sleep.

Of course, it can be hard to have your body change at a slower or faster rate than your friends' bodies. If how fast or slow your body is changing is upsetting you, talk to an adult you trust.

Note- If you're developing slower or faster than you think you should, your body may just be changing at its own natural rate. It's a good idea to let your doctor know if you start puberty before age 8. Also let your doctor know if you don't have any signs of puberty by the time you're 14. Your doctor can check whether a medical problem is involved.

During puberty your body may seem very different from what you're used to, and you might feel uncomfortable or shy about it. Remember that everyone goes through these changes — it's just part of life — and every girl grows at her own pace.

During puberty, it's common to struggle with body image, or how you feel about your body. This can be especially hard when models in magazines have bodies that seem "perfect." But a lot of what you see in magazines and online is either fake or unhealthy.

If you think you or a friend may have a problem with body image or an eating disorder, talk to a parent, a doctor, or another adult you trust. Help is available, and it's important to get treated. You can get better!

Remember, measure yourself by your great traits and loving heart — not by the size and shape of your body!

Changes to Your Breasts

The biggest and most notable change you will experience on the outside of your body (besides your height) that will be noticeable to yourself and others will be your breasts. So, let's cover that topic in detail.

Throughout puberty, you will experience changes in your breasts. The first change is developing a very small bump under the nipple. Early on, you may also notice that your breasts feel a little itchy or achy. Later on, they also may feel tender or sore during your period.

Keep in mind that it is very common for your two breasts to be different sizes, especially as they first start to grow. But don't worry; other people can't tell that your breasts are different sizes. Give your body time to grow at its own rate and in its own way. Vitamins, herbal teas, and creams — even exercises — won't change the size of your breasts. So, just exercise patience.

Most of the changes your breasts will go through are normal. Let your doctor know if you find a lump or have a pain that you are not sure about. Although lumps are common in young women, keep in mind that it is very rare for the lumps to be cancer.

Wearing a bra can help support and protect your breasts. If you find that exercise is not as comfortable when your breasts start to grow, try wearing a sports bra with a snug fit for support.

Are you having a hard time finding a bra that fits well? Often, you can get help in a department store or special bra store. There are certain steps people there can take for measuring your body to get a good fit.

It's natural for girls to wonder about their breasts: Are they too big? Too small? If your breasts are large, they may get you unwanted attention. If they're small, you may worry that they'll never grow. Remember that your breasts don't need to look like your friend's breasts or a magazine model's breasts. The world would be boring if everyone looked the same!

Body Hair

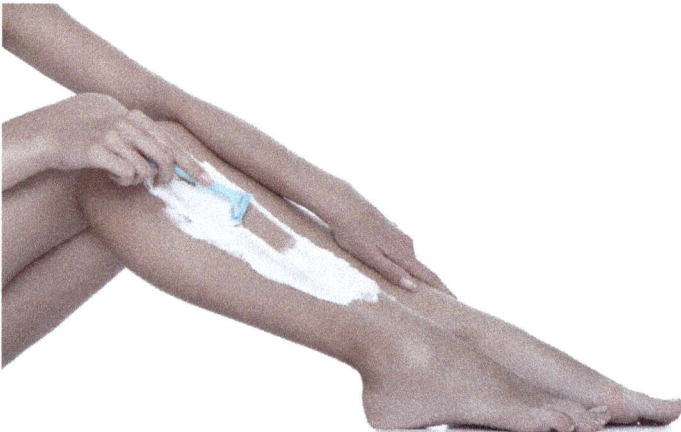

Even before you get your first period, you will likely see new hair growing in your pubic area, under your arms, and on your legs. The hair may start out light and there won't be a lot of it, but then it will grow darker and thicker, as you go through the stages of puberty. Hair in the pubic area starts near the opening and spreads up in a V shape over time.

Body hair is normal, and some people think it looks cool. Lots of women and girls remove body hair from places such as their legs and underarms, although there is no real health reason to do so.

If you are thinking about removing hair for the first time, it makes sense to talk to your parents or guardians. They may have an opinion about how old you should be to start removing hair or advice on ways to do it.

Ways to get rid of hair

Removing body hair can cause skin irritation, cuts, and other problems. Some parts of your body, like areas around your eyes and vagina, can be especially sensitive. Here are some tips to help prevent problems when using some popular ways to remove body hair.

Shaving

Try shaving in the shower when your skin is soft.

Use a shaving cream or gel.

Change razors often because a sharp blade helps prevent cuts.

Shave in the direction the hair grows.

To avoid spreading infections, don't share razors.

Hair removal creams, gels, and liquids (depilatories)

These use chemicals to make the hair melt, and the chemicals can irritate your skin.

Follow the directions carefully, and leave the product on only for the recommended amount of time.

Don't use these near your eyes or on skin that is already cut or irritated.

These sometimes can cause rashes, burns, and other skin problems, so it is a good idea to test a product on a small area the first time you use it. You might want to avoid these products if you tend to have sensitive skin.

Waxing

Waxing involves putting cold or hot wax on skin where you want hair to be removed. A cloth is used to pull off the wax and the hair. Waxing can hurt, and it may irritate your skin.

You can buy waxes to use yourself, or you can go to a salon professional for waxing. If you wax yourself, make sure to follow all directions that come with the product.

You might avoid waxing if you have sensitive skin. Also, avoid waxing skin that is sunburned, chapped, irritated, or has moles or warts on it.

It can be a good idea to do a test on a small area for allergic reaction or irritation.

Changes in Your Mind

During puberty, changes don't happen only to your body — changes happen in your mind, too.

You are able to understand more complex matters.

You are starting to make more of your own moral choices.

You know more about who you are and what your likes and dislikes are.

You may have some new, strong emotions.

The teen years can seem like an emotional roller coaster, with worries about your changing looks, the demands of school, and pressure to fit in. You might feel alone on this ride, but everyone struggles with it. And some of your experiences have to do with the physical changes of this age, including shifts in your hormones and a brain that's developing just like your body is.

A new you

Even though this can be a stressful time, it is also a great chance to figure out who you are, what you care about, and how to value and respect the person you are becoming!

If you are feeling overwhelmed by some of the changes you are going through, talking can help. Don't be afraid to go to a parent, school counselor, or other adult you trust. They were young once too, and they really do understand what you are going through because they already went through it. Most teenagers tend to feel more comfortable speaking with a peer. But, ask yourself, "Does my friend know any more about this than I do?" If you answer, "No," to that question, then find someone else to speak to.

Getting your period

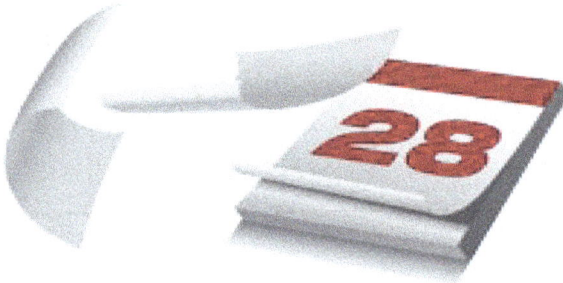

Starting your period — or menstruation — is a major part of puberty and means you can now become pregnant. Some girls find getting their periods very exciting, and others feel uncomfortable about it. It definitely can take a little getting used to! But lots of women come to see their periods as a wonderful sign that their bodies are healthy and working the way they're supposed to.

Understanding Your Period

What comes out during your period is the blood and tissue that build up as the lining of your uterus each month. Your period flow can be light, heavy, or in between. Sometimes menstrual blood also will be different shades of red, from light to dark. You may see some dark clumps or clots of blood, which is normal.

Your period may be heavy the first day or so each time and then decrease on later days. Periods usually last between three and five days. It is normal to have periods that are shorter or longer, up to seven days. It is also normal if your periods are not the same number of days each month, especially in the first years.

If you think your period is too heavy or have other concerns about your period, please see your personal physician, specifically a gynecologist.

At what age do you get your first period?

Usually, girls get their periods between ages 12 and 14, but it can happen years before or after that. Don't worry if you get your period later or earlier than your friends get theirs — that happens a lot. If you haven't gotten your period by age 15 (or within three years of when your breasts started to grow), talk to your parents or guardians, your doctor, or another adult you trust.

What causes your period?

Natural body chemicals, or hormones, cause your ovaries to release one egg about once a month. Most months, the egg and the lining of your uterus come out of your vagina as your period. This is part of your menstrual cycle. This cycle is what makes it possible for a woman to have a baby. During sexual intercourse, the egg can get fertilized by a male's sperm and then attach to the lining of the uterus and develop into a baby.

Does your period come each month?

Menstrual cycles take place over about one month (around 21 to 34 days), but each woman's cycle is different. Many women have a cycle that lasts 28 days. Some women may have cycles as long as 45 days. The cycle includes not just your period, but the rise and fall of hormones and other body changes that take place over the month.

Keep in mind that your periods may not be regular at first. You may have two in one month, or have a month without a period at all. Also, at first your period may last just a couple of days in some months and up to a week in other months. Periods will become more regular over time.

To learn about your own pattern, it's a good idea to keep track of your periods on a calendar or app. Keeping track lets you:

Get a sense of when to expect your next period

Know if you missed a period (if it comes on a regular schedule)

Have a record of your period schedule and when your last one came to share with your gynecologist or other health care provider

When you chart your cycle, remember that it starts with the first day of one period and goes until the first day of the next period.

Getting Enough Sleep

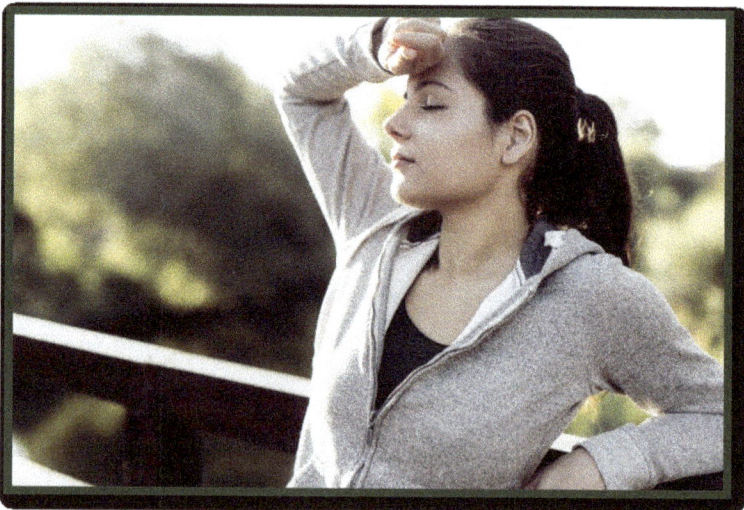

Sleep may seem like a waste of time when you have so much going on. But sleep can help you do better in school or work, stress less, and generally be more pleasant to have

around. Sound good? Now consider some possible effects of
not getting enough sleep:

Feeling angry or depressed

Having trouble learning, remembering, and thinking
clearly

Having more accidents, including when driving or using
machines

Getting sick more often

Feeling less motivated

Possibly gaining weight

Having lower self-esteem

Tips for better sleep

**Go to bed and wake up at the same time
every day** — even on the weekends!

Exercise regularly. Don't exercise at the
expense of sleep, though.

Don't eat a lot close to bedtime. Food can
give you a burst of energy.

Avoid bright lights right before bed,
including the ones that come from the TV or
the computer. Sleep in a dark room. Darkness
tells your body it's time for sleep.

Sleep in a slightly cool room. If you can't
control the temperature, try using fewer
blankets or dressing lightly.

Follow a bedtime routine. If you do the same things each night before bed, your body will know it's time for sleep. Take a warm bath or shower. Or, drink a glass of milk.

Wake up to bright light. Light tells your body it's time to get up.

Listen to your body. If you're feeling tired, go to sleep. If you can't fall asleep within 20 minutes of going to bed, get up and do something else until you feel sleepy.

Avoid caffeine. That means cutting back on coffee, soda, chocolate, and energy drinks — or at least trying not to have any in the afternoon.

Don't nap for longer than an hour or take naps too close to bedtime.

Don't stay up all night studying. Try doing some each night instead. If you pull an all-nighter, you may be too tired to do well on your test.

Set aside time to relax for about an hour before bed. If your tasks have you worried, write them down to get them off your mind.

Remove computers, phones, and other gadgets. Put your cell phone out of your room, so you won't be tempted to use it, and so texts and calls won't wake you.

If these tips don't help, tell your parents or guardians. You also might talk to your doctor or nurse.

How much is enough?

Experts say most teens need a little more than nine hours of sleep each night, while adults only need 6 or 7. Only a tiny number get that much, though. Here are some ways to see if you are getting enough sleep:

Do you have trouble getting up in the morning?

Do you have trouble focusing?

Do you sometimes fall asleep during class?

If you answered yes to these questions, try using the tips above for getting better sleep. Also keep in mind that good sleep isn't just about the number of hours you are in bed. If you wake up a lot in the night, snore, or have headaches, you may not be getting enough quality sleep to keep you fresh and healthy.

Looking and Feeling Your Best

Most of us want to make a good impression and care about how we look. So, it makes sense that we put a fair amount of effort into things like our hair and skin. But a lot of looking and feeling your best comes from taking good care of yourself and having a healthy self-image. An inner glow and a feeling of confidence help to make you shine on the outside!

Do you feel pressure to look "good"? One great way to deal with this is to refuse to compare yourself to girls in TV shows, magazines, and movies. They have whole crews of professionals — and camera and computer tricks — to help them look good.

Remember, everyone young lady has something beautiful about her! If your friends start complaining that they are fat or ugly, try saying what's beautiful about them — inside and out. Or, you could just try changing the subject.

If you spend a lot of time feeling bad about your looks, you might have a problem with your body image. Talking to an adult you trust can help a lot, so don't be shy about your worries. As your body changes, you can feel a lot more comfortable and confident if you've got the information you need.

Sweating

You might think that you are only supposed to sweat when you are hot, but once you hit puberty, you will also sweat when you are nervous. Your sweat glands, which are in places like your armpits, become more active during the teen years. That means you will sweat more, and your sweat will have a smell.

Don't panic! Sweat and smell are normal parts of becoming an adult. Sweating also does an important job — it helps cool your body when you are hot.

You can follow some simple tips to keep from smelling bad:

> Shower or take a bath every day, making sure to wash your underarms, pubic area, and bottom.
>
> Use a deodorant, which helps get rid of smells, or an antiperspirant, which decreases sweating, or a product that has both of these in it.
>
> Talk to your doctor if these things do not work or you are worried about smelling bad.

Bad Breath

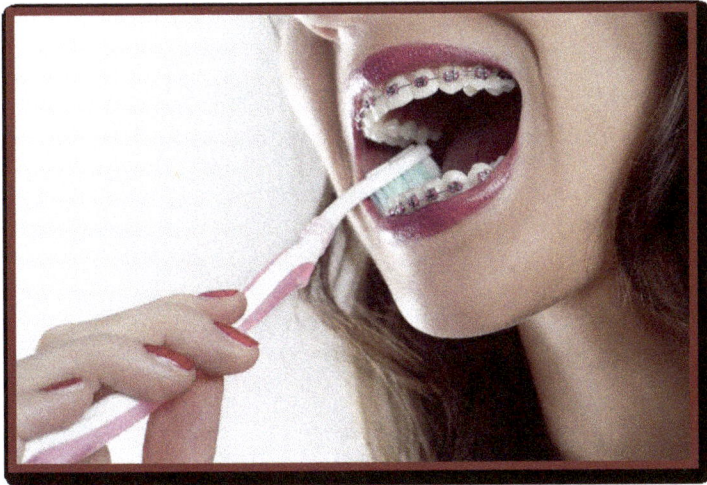

When you open your mouth to talk, you probably want your friends to think about what you're saying — and not about what you ate for lunch. But certain strong-smelling foods like onions and garlic can cause bad breath. Smoking can cause bad breath also. Furthermore, bacteria that grow on bits of food that get stuck between your teeth can cause bad breath. Lots of people have bad breath at some point. Don't worry! There are steps you can take to keep your mouth fresh and healthy.

Tips for preventing bad breath:

Brush your teeth (and tongue!) for at least two minutes twice a day with fluoride toothpaste, especially after meals and at bedtime.

Ask your dentist how to floss correctly. Flossing can remove tiny bits of food that can rot and smell bad.

Replace your toothbrush every three to four months.

Visit your dentist twice a year. He or she will help keep your teeth and your mouth healthy.

Eat smart. Avoid foods and drinks that can leave behind strong smells, like cabbage, garlic, raw onions, and coffee. If you're trying to lose weight, remember that not eating enough or cutting out certain foods (such as carbohydrates) can cause bad breath.

Don't smoke! You'll smell sweeter — and be a lot healthier.

Drink enough fluids. Drinking helps wash away tiny bits of food and bacteria, which can smell bad.

If your bad breath doesn't go away, be sure to talk to your dentist, doctor, or nurse. It could be a sign of a medical problem, such as a sinus infection or gum disease. You may feel a little funny talking about bad breath, but it's very common, and you can get help.

Tips for keeping your mouth healthy:

A lot of the tips for keeping your mouth healthy are the same as the tips for stopping bad breath, such as brushing and flossing. Below are some more tips for good oral hygiene, which is just a fancy way to say taking care of your teeth and mouth. Do you feel like they are a pain? Well, they are a lot less of a pain than the dentist's drill!

> **Eat smart.** Avoid sugary foods and drinks. This helps prevent damage to your teeth and is great for your overall health.
>
> **Brush after sweets.** If you eat or drink sugary items, try to brush right after. If you can't brush, at least rinse your mouth with water.
>
> **Definitely don't smoke.** Smoking doesn't just smell bad and stain your teeth. It also can increase your risk of gum disease and tooth decay.

Acne

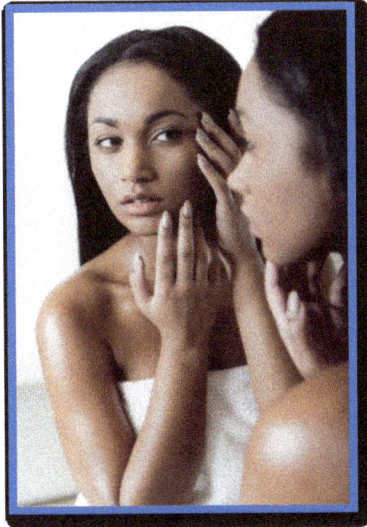

Whether you call them pimples, zits, or acne, lots of teens find skin problems confusing and upsetting. But you can understand what's going on with your skin and what you can do about it. Here's a closer look at acne, from causes to cures.

What causes acne?

Acne happens when your pores get clogged with dead skin and oil. Acne often starts during puberty because your body is making more oil and a certain type of bacteria starts growing in pores. Acne can show up on your face, but you can get it on your back, chest, and other places too.

Whiteheads develop when a pore gets plugged with oil and dead skin cells.

Blackheads happen when this plugged-up substance comes to the surface of the skin. The black is *not* dirt.

Pustules (what is often called pimples) develop when a plugged-up pore gets inflamed and filled with pus.

Cystic acne happens when a plugged pore breaks deep inside the skin. Nodules (large, inflamed bumps) or cysts (pus-filled bumps) form and often look like larger pimples. Sometimes they can cause scars and pain.

Remember that acne is common among teens — you're not the only one dealing with it. Why do some people have more acne than others? Some people just have more sensitive skin. Also, acne can run in your family, so if your mom or dad had it, you may, too. Severe acne sometimes can be a sign of hormone problems, so ask your doctor if you're concerned.

What can make acne worse?

Several things might make your acne worse, including: Using oil-based makeup instead of "non-comedogenic" ones that may not clog pores

Using suntan oil and oil-based hair products, including pomade

Your period

Picking at your pimples

Scrubbing your skin too hard

Tanning

Stress

Wearing things that press against your skin, such as spandex and baseball caps

Working at a job that involves frying foods

Acne treatments

There are lots of options for dealing with acne. Here is some helpful info:

First, you can wash your face twice a day with a mild cleanser.

You might also wash it after you sweat a lot. (But washing it more than two or three times a day can irritate your skin.)

You can also lessen the oils on your face by keeping your hair clean if it's oily.

You can buy over-the-counter acne medication.

These gels, lotions, and creams fight acne with ingredients like benzoyl peroxide and salicylic acid. They generally are helpful for mild acne.

Follow all directions carefully to avoid possible problems. It's a good idea to test the product on a small spot if you've never used it before. Then wait three days. If the medicine doesn't cause problems for you, go ahead and use it on other areas.

You may need to use these products regularly for several weeks before they start to work. If they don't lessen your acne after two months, ask your doctor for help.

Stop using the product and tell your doctor if you have a bad skin reaction to any of these products. Stop using the product and call 911 or go to the nearest hospital emergency department right away if you have any of these: a tight feeling in your throat, feeling faint, having trouble breathing, or swelling of your eyes, face, lips, or tongue. These are signs of an allergic reaction that is rare but that is dangerous.

If over-the-counter medicines don't work well, your doctor can give you prescription medicine.

These medicines could include an antibiotic cream or a gel or cream made with a type of medicine called a retinoid.

Prescription treatments also could include an antibiotic pill or possibly even a birth control pill.

If you use a retinoid or antibiotic pill, make sure to stay in the shade and use sunscreen because these increase the risk of sunburn.

What doesn't cause acne?

You may have heard that eating lots of greasy foods can cause acne. Researchers say that's not true. Of course, it's still smart to skip unhealthy behaviors just to take good care of yourself.

Food for thought: Researchers are exploring whether a certain type of food might increase acne. These are items like white bread, cake, and cookies that are called high-glycemic foods (which means they raise the level of sugar in your blood). More research is needed, but if you think your diet may be affecting your acne, talk to your doctor.

Seeing the doctor

As you get older, it's a good idea to get more involved in taking care of your own health. Getting involved with your health will not only help protect your body — it can make you feel really proud of yourself!

Of course, you don't have to take care of your health by yourself. Work together with caring adults like your parents or guardians to protect your great, growing body.

Work closely with your doctor — and not just when you're sick but also to prevent any problems. Your doctor will tell you how often you should come in for a checkup, which is usually once a year.

Your doctor or other health care provider can help you with everything from sports injuries to immunizations. You can start getting more involved by asking the doctor for tips in areas like nutrition, exercise, and safety.

If you have a health problem, your physician can help you stay strong both emotionally and physically.

Tough Topics

Your doctor can be a great resource for teen health topics that can be a little rough for you. These might include:

How fast your body should develop during puberty

Feeling unhappy for no obvious reason

Worries about your eating habits

The whole complicated topic of sex

Pressure to smoke, drink alcohol, or use drugs

You may feel a little embarrassed to raise these issues, but doctors and nurses have heard about all this before — and they want to give you the support you need to stay healthy and happy.

(Information courtesy of Office of Women's Health, 2017)

NOTES

_____

_____

_____

_____

_____

_____

_____

_____

_____

_____

_____

_____

_____

Chapter Two

Knowing and Accepting Yourself
(Self-Esteem)

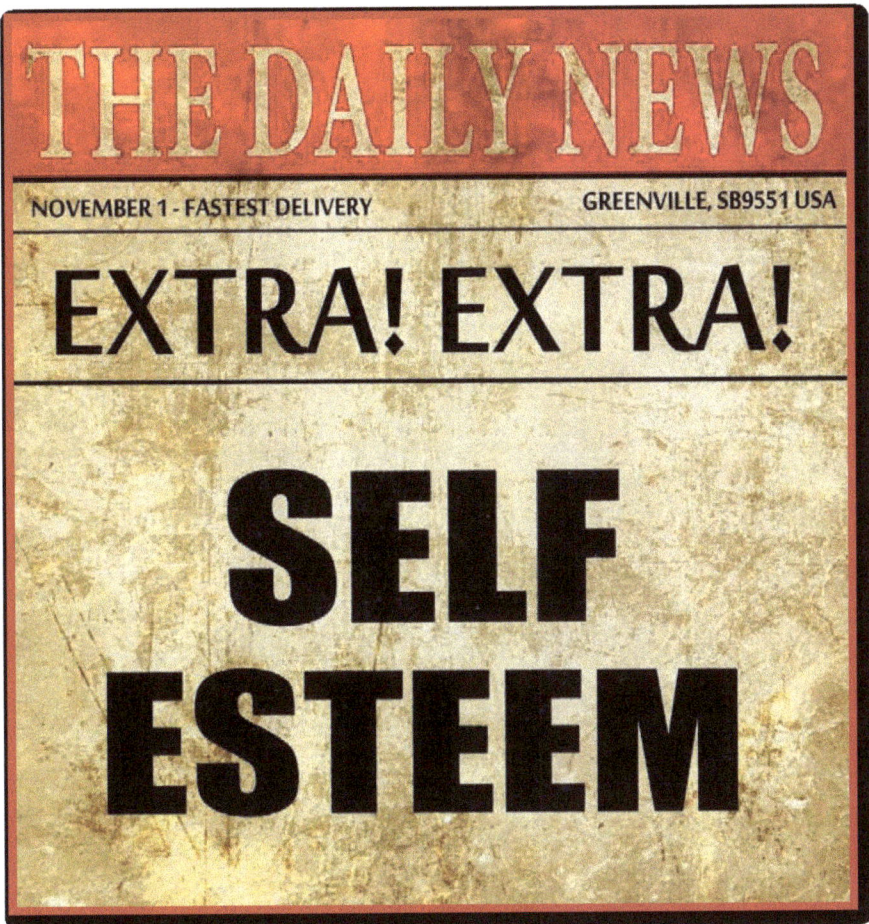

Beyond the Reflection

Looking in the mirror, what do you see?
The eyes of a monster, the hair of a beast.
A bump, a lump, an excuse for a nose.
Eyelashes to short, eyebrows that grow.

Shoulders broad, legs too skinny,
a smile with lines too deep and wimpy.
Cheeks rather puffy, and a scowl, rather scruffy.

Now mirror my eyes, what do I see?
Eyes of an angel, hair of a Greek.
A curve, a shimmy, a button nose.
Eyelashes that accent eyebrows of pose.
Shoulders of confidence, legs considered sexy,
A smile with lines of laughter and living,
Cheeks so cute, and an expression of love.

What monster do you speak of?
A beast? I see none.
Before me, and angel of wings,
a friend, and a loved one.

What ugliness is this?
What Flaw is that?
Shush, shut your lips,
you are blind as a bat.

You strut,
You dance,
You shout and sing,
to me you are beauty,
Who is so nasty as to attack your self-esteem?
Their words, my friend, are not worth listening.

© 2012 Tiffany Ruggles

Nothing is more important than how you feel and what you think about yourself. A high opinion about yourself and who you are and what you do and basically a love for yourself is also one of the things that people often miss or have too little of in today's society.

But why is building and being able to maintain high self-esteem so important?

- **Life becomes simpler and lighter.** When you like or love yourself more, things simply become easier. You won't make mountains out of molehills (or out of plain air) nearly as often anymore. You won't drag yourself down or beat yourself up over simple mistakes or over not reaching a perfect and inhuman standard.

- **You'll have more inner stability.** When you like yourself more and your opinion of yourself goes up, then you'll stop trying so eagerly to get validation and attention from other people. And, you become less needy, and your inner life becomes much less of an emotional rollercoaster based on what people may think or say about you today or this week. This does not mean people's negative comments won't hurt. They will. But, you won't be dependent upon outside approval or accolades.

- **Less self-sabotage.** Most people's worst enemy is themselves. By raising and keeping your self-esteem up, you'll feel more deserving of good things in life. And so, you'll go after them more often and with more motivation. And when you get them, you'll be a lot less likely to self-sabotage in subtle or not so subtle ways.

- **You'll be more attractive in any relationship.** With better self-esteem, you'll get the benefits listed above. You'll be more stable and able to handle tough times better. You'll be less needy and more of a natural giver. Being with you becomes simpler and a lighter experience with a lot less drama, arguments or fights based on little or nothing. And all of this is attractive in any relationship, no matter if it is with a friend, at work, or with a partner.

- **You'll be happier.** Self-satisfaction leads to outer happiness and inner joy.

Now, the question is- How does one improve her self-esteem in a practical way?

Here, I would like to share twelve of the most powerful tips and habits that have been proven for improving and maintaining self-esteem, even through the rough days and tough months.

1. Say "Stop" to your inner critic.

A good place to start with raising your self-esteem is by learning how to handle and to replace the voice of your own inner critic. We all have an inner critic. It can spur you on to get things done or to do things to gain acceptance from the people in your life. But, at the same time, it will drag your self-esteem down. This inner voice whispers or shouts destructive thoughts in your mind. For example,

- You are lazy and sloppy; now get to work.

- You aren't good at your job at all, and someone will figure that out and throw you out.
- You are worse or uglier than your friend/co-worker/partner.

No matter how loud the inner voice, you don't have to accept the negative comments. There are ways to minimize that critical voice and to replace it with more helpful thoughts. You can change how you view yourself.

One way to do so is simply to say, "Stop," whenever the critic pipes up in your mind. You can do this by creating a stop-word or stop-phrase. As the critic says something, in your mind, shout: "STOP!" Or, use my favorite: "No, no, no! We are not going there!" Or, come up with a phrase or word that you like that stops the train of the thought driven by the inner critic.

Then refocus your thoughts to something more constructive, like planning what you want to eat for dinner, or your tactic for the next soccer game. In the long run, it also helps a lot to find better ways to motivate yourself than listening to your inner critic. So let's move on to that...

2. Use healthier motivation habits.

To make the inner critic less useful for yourself and that voice weaker and at the same time motivate yourself to take action and raise your self-esteem, it certainly helps to have healthy motivation habits.

To replace and fill up much of the place the inner critic holds in your mind are the following:

- **Remind yourself of the benefits.** A simple but powerful way to motivate yourself and to keep that motivation up daily is to write down the deeply felt benefits you will get from following this new path or reaching a goal. For example, getting into better shape and having more energy for your kids and the people close to you. Or making more money and through that being able to travel with the love of your life and experience wonderful new things together. When your list is done, save it, and put it somewhere where you will see it every day, such as in your workspace or on your fridge.

- **Refocus on doing what YOU really, really like to do.** When you really, really like doing something, the motivation to do that thing tends to come pretty automatically. When you really want something in life, it also becomes easier to push through any inner resistance you feel. If you lose your motivation, ask yourself: "Am I doing what I really want to do?" If not and if possible, then refocus and start working on that very important thing instead.

After you have used your stop-word or phrase, focus on one of these techniques. Over time, it will become a habit, and your inner critic will pop up a lot less often.

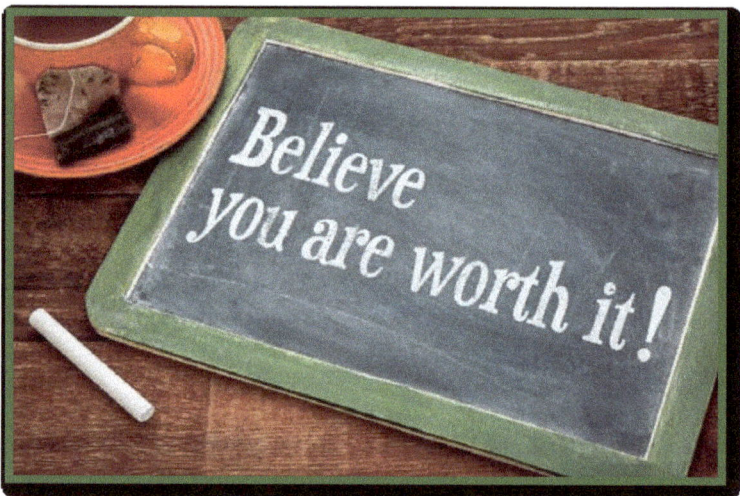

3. Take a 2 minute self-appreciation break.

This is a very simple and fun habit. And, if you spend just two minutes on it every day for a month, it can make a huge difference.

Here's what you do:

Take a deep breath, slow down, and ask yourself this question: "What are three things I can appreciate about myself?"

A few examples that others have come up with are:

- Help quite a few people each day through what I write.
- Can make people laugh and forget about their troubles.
- Am very thoughtful and caring when it comes to our cats.

These things don't have to be big things. Maybe just that you listened fully for a few minutes to someone who needed it today. That you took a healthy walk or bike ride after work. That you are a caring and kind person in many situations. These short breaks do not only build self-esteem in the long run but can also turn a negative mood around and reload you with a lot of positive energy again.

4. Write down three things in the evening that you can appreciate about yourself.

This is a variation of the habit above and combining the two of them can be extra powerful for two boosts in self-esteem a day. Or, you may simply prefer to use this variation at the end of your day when you have some free time for yourself to spare. Ask yourself: What are three things I can appreciate about myself?

Write down your answers every evening in a journal made out of paper or on your computer/smart phone. A nice extra benefit of writing it down is that after a few weeks, you can read through all the answers to get a good self-esteem boost and change in perspective on days when you may need it the most.

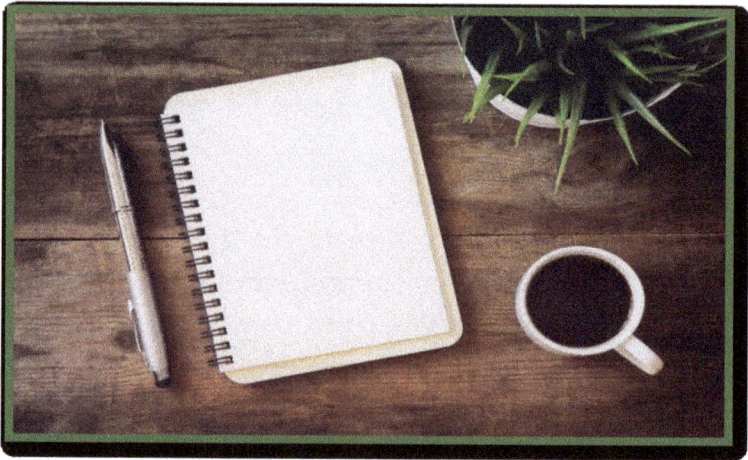

5. Do the right thing.

When you do what you believe is the right thing to do, you raise and strengthen your self-esteem. It might be a small thing like getting up from the couch and going to the gym. It could be being understanding instead of judgmental in a situation or to stop feeling sorry for yourself and focus on the opportunities and gratitude for what you actually have.

It is not always easy to do. But keep focus on it, and do it as best you can, making a big difference both in the results you get and for how you think about yourself.

One tip that makes it easier to stay consistent with doing the right thing is to try to take a few such actions early in the day. For example, giving someone a compliment, eating a healthy breakfast and working out. This sets the tone for the rest of your day.

6. Replace the perfectionism.

Being a perfectionist can be as destructive as having low self-esteem. It can paralyze you from taking action because you become so afraid of not living up to a particular standard. Then, you procrastinate, and you do not get the results you want. This will make your self-esteem sink.

Or, you take action but are never or very rarely satisfied with what you accomplished and your own performance. Then, your opinion and feelings about yourself become more and more negative, and your motivation to take action plummets.

How can you overcome perfectionism?

Remember that buying into myths of perfection will hurt you and the people in your life. This simple reminder that life is not like in a movie, a song or a book can be good reality check whenever you are daydreaming of perfection. Because reality can clash with your expectations when they are out of this world and harm or even possibly lead to the end of relationships, jobs, projects and so on.

7. Handle mistakes and failures in a more positive way.

If you go outside of your comfort zone and try to accomplish anything that is truly meaningful, then you will stumble and fall along the way. And that is okay. It is normal. It is what people that did something that truly mattered have done throughout all ages, even if we don't always hear about it as much as we hear about their successes.

So remember that. And when you stumble try this:

- **Be your own best friend.** Instead of beating yourself up, ask yourself: "How would my friend/parent support me and help me in this situation?" Then, do things and talk to yourself like he/she would. It keeps you from falling into a pit of despair and helps you to be more constructive after the first initial pain of a mistake or failure starts to dissipate.
- **Find the upside.** Another way to be more constructive in this kind of situation is to focus on optimism and opportunities. So ask yourself: "What is one thing I can learn from this? And what is one opportunity I can find in

this situation?" This will help you to change your viewpoint and hopefully not hit the same bump a little further down the road.

8. Be kinder towards other people.

When you are kinder towards others, you tend to treat and think of yourself in a kinder way as well. And the way you treat other people is how they tend to treat you in the long run. So, focus on being kind in your daily life.

You can for example:

- Just be there and listen as you let someone vent.
- Hold open the door for the next person.
- Let someone into your lane while driving.
- Encourage a friend or a family member when he/she is uncertain or unmotivated.
- Take a few minutes help someone out in a practical way.

9. Try something new.

When you try something new or challenge yourself in a small or bigger way and go outside of your comfort zone, your opinion of yourself goes up. You may not have done whatever you did in a spectacular or great way, but you at least tried instead of sitting on your hands and doing nothing. That is something to appreciate about yourself, and it can help you come alive as you get out of a rut.

So, go outside of your comfort zone regularly. Don't expect anything. Just tell yourself you will try something out. Later, you can do the same thing a few more times and improve your own performance. And as always, if it feels too scary or uncomfortable, don't beat yourself up. Take a smaller step forward instead by gently nudging yourself into motion.

10. Stop falling into the comparison trap.

When you compare your life, yourself, and what you have to other people's lives and what they have, you have a destructive habit on your hands. You can never win by doing this. There is always someone who has more or is better than you at something in the world. There are always people ahead of you. So, replace that habit with something better. Look at how far you have come so far instead. Compare yourself to yourself. Focus on yourself, your results, and how you can and have improved your results. This will both motivate you and raise your self-esteem.

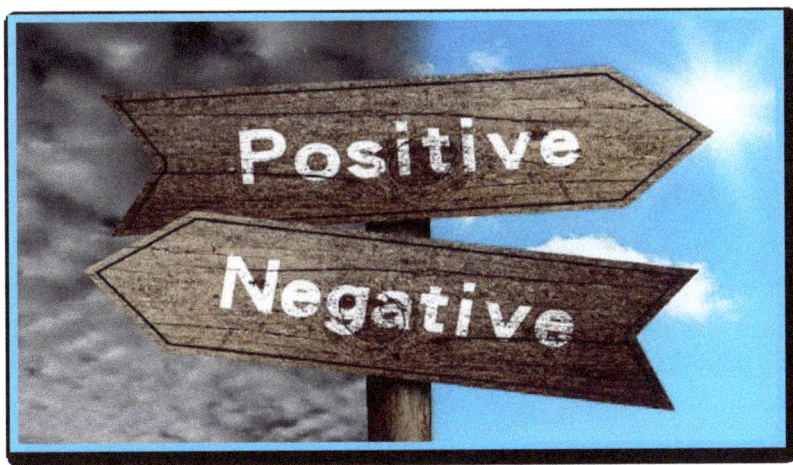

11. Spend more time with supportive people (and less time with destructive people).

Even if you focus on being kinder towards other people (and yourself) and on replacing a perfectionist attitude, it will be hard to keep your self-esteem up if the most important influences in your life drag it down on a daily or weekly basis.

Make changes in the input you get. Choose to spend less time with people who are nervous perfectionists, unkind or unsupportive of your dreams or goals. And spend more time with positive, uplifting people who have more human and kinder standards and ways of thinking about things.

And think about what you read, listen to and watch, too. Spend less time on an internet forum, with reading a magazine or watching a TV-show if you feel it makes you unsure of yourself and if it makes you feel more negatively towards yourself.

Spend the time you used to spend on this information source on for example reading books, blogs, websites and listening to podcasts that help you and that make you feel good about yourself.

12. Remember the whys of high self-esteem.

What is a simple way to stay consistent with doing something? As mentioned above: to remember the most important reasons why you are doing it.

So, remind yourself of the whys at the start of this chapter to help yourself to stay motivated to work on your self-esteem and to make it an essential priority. Doing this simple thing and keeping these powerful reasons in mind has done wonders for many people. I hope it can do the same for you.

(Adapted from Edberg)

NOTES

_____

_____

_____

_____

_____

_____

_____

_____

_____

_____

_____

_____

_____

Chapter Three

Setting Goals: Short and Long Term

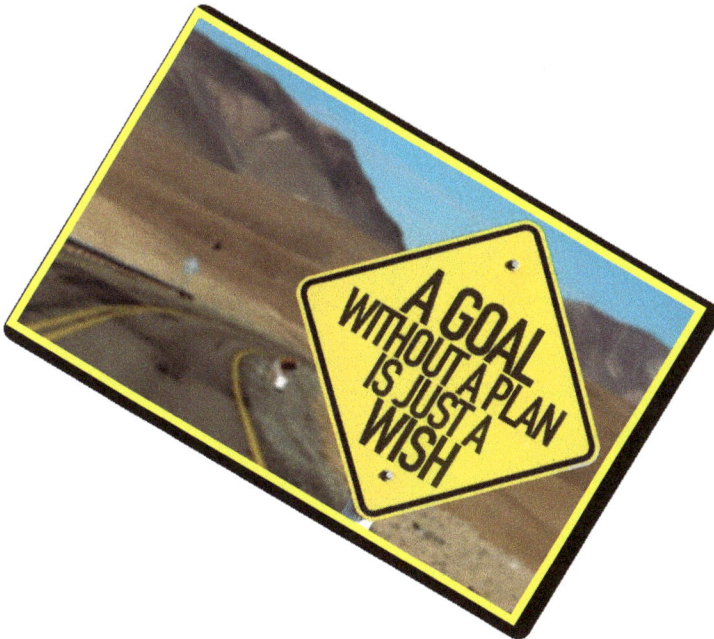

My Goals

Once I had a little dream,
All shiny, bright and new.
And for many years its seemed
That little dream just grew.

But other dreams came into play
And crowded out the one.
Many lasted but a day
And most were left undone.

Soon life became the only goal.
And dreams were left forgotten,
Just gettin' by soon took its toll;
My dream chest lat a'rottin'.

I sat today and looked at life
The half-way point now reached.
It seems I have to catch my breath;
Did I practice what I preached?

How many years are left to me,
Before my song is sung?
And what will I accomplished see,
And what will be left undone?

And so I dusted of the dream,
And polished it anew.
And if God wills, it realized will be.
Before my life is through.

by Geri Hausler

Method 1

Setting Achievable Goals

Determine your life goals. Ask yourself some important questions about what you want for your life. What do you want to achieve: today, in a year, in your lifetime? The answers to this question can be as general as "I want to be happy," or "I want to help people." Consider what you hope to attain 10, 15, or 20 years from now.

- A career life goal might be to open your own business. A fitness goal might be to become fit. A personal goal might be to have a family one day. These goals can be incredibly broad.

Examples of Specific Goals

Family

I want to eat at the dinner table twice a week

I want to tell a family member that I appreciate them once a week

I want to prepare vegetables for every family meal that I cook

Career

I want to apply to a new job once a week

I want to ask for more responsibility

I want to ask someone I admire to coffee once a month to ask for advice

Education

I want to learn how to code html

I want to learn basic Spanish for my vacation

I want to start researching graduate schools

Health

I want to start meditating for 10 minutes on the weekends

I want to try hiking to see if I enjoy it

I want to skip dessert on week nights

Break the big picture down into smaller and more specific goals. Consider areas of your life that you either want to change or that you feel you would like to develop with time. Areas might include: career, finances, family, education, or health. Begin to ask yourself questions about what you'd like to achieve in each area and how you would like to approach it within a five year time frame.

- For the life goal "I want to be fit," you might make the smaller goals "I want to eat more healthily" and "I want to run a marathon."

- For the life goal "I want to open my own business," the smaller goals may be "I want to learn to manage a business effectively" and "I want to open an independent book store."

Write goals for the short term. Now that you know roughly what you want to accomplish within a few years, make concrete goals for you to begin working on now. Give yourself a deadline within a reasonable time frame (no more than a year for short-term goals).

- Writing your goals will make them harder to ignore, consequently making you accountable for them.
- To become fit, your first goals may be to eat more vegetables and to run a 5k.
- To open your own business, your first goals may be to take a bookkeeping class and to find the perfect location for your bookstore.

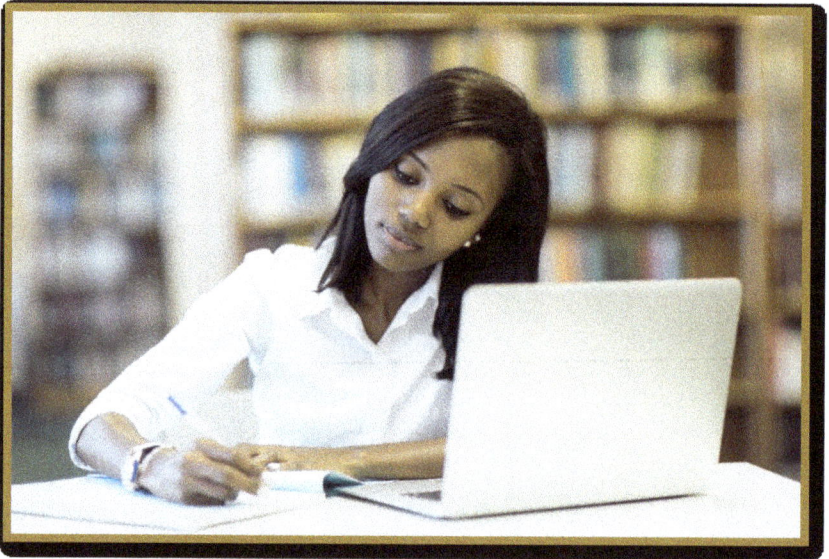

Make your goals smaller steps that move you towards larger life goals. Basically, you need to decide why you're setting this goal for yourself and what it will accomplish. Some good questions to ask yourself when figuring this out are: Does it seem worthwhile? Is now the right time for this? Does this match my needs?

- For example, while a short-term fitness goal might be to take up a new sport within six months, ask yourself if that will help you reach your bigger goal of running a marathon. If not, consider changing the short term goal to something that will be a step towards meeting the life goal.

Adjust your goals periodically. You may find yourself set in your ways concerning broad life goals, but take the time to re-evaluate your smaller goals. Are you accomplishing them according to your time frame? Are they still necessary to keep you on track towards your larger life goals? Allow yourself the flexibility to adjust your goals.

- To become fit, you may have mastered running 5K races. Perhaps after you have run a few and worked on improving your personal best times, you should adjust your goal from "run a 5K" to "run a 10K." Eventually, you can move to "run a half marathon," then "run a marathon."

- To open your own business, after completing the first goals of taking a bookkeeping class and finding a location, you may set new goals to obtain a business loan to purchase a space and to apply for the proper business licensing through your local government. Afterwards, you can move towards buying (or leasing) the space, then obtaining the books you need, hiring staff, and opening your doors to business. Eventually, you may even work towards opening a second location!

Method 2
Practicing Effective Goal Strategies

Make your goals specific. When setting goals, they should answer the highly specific questions of who, what, where, when, and why. For each specific goal you make, you should ask yourself why it is a goal and how it helps your life goals.

- To become fit (which is very general), you have created the more specific goal "run a marathon," which begins with the short-term goal "run a 5K." When you set each short-term goal—such as running a 5K, you can answer the questions: Who?

Me. What? Run a 5K. Where? At a local park. When? In 6 weeks. Why? To work towards my goal of running a marathon.

- To open your own business, you have created the short term goal "take a bookkeeping class." This can answer the questions: Who? Me. What? Take a bookkeeping class. Where? At the Library. When? Every Saturday for 5 weeks. Why? To learn how to manage a budget for my business.

Create measurable goals. In order for us to track our progress, goals should be quantifiable. "I'm going to walk more" is far more difficult to track and measure than "Every day I'm going to walk around the track 16 times." Essentially, you'll need a few ways of determining if you're reaching your goal.

- "Run a 5K" is a measurable goal. You know for certain when you have done it. You may need to set the even shorter-term goal of "run at least 3 miles, 3 times every week" to work towards your first 5K. After your first 5K, a measurable goal would be "run another 5K in one month, but take 4 minutes off of my time."

- Likewise, "take a bookkeeping class" is measurable because it is a specific class that you will sign up to take and go to every week. A less measurable version would be "learn about bookkeeping," which is vague because it's difficult to know when you're "finished" learning about bookkeeping.

Be realistic with your goals. It is important to evaluate your situation honestly and recognize which goals are realistic and which are a little far-fetched. Ask yourself if you have the all the things you need to complete your goal (skill, resources, time, knowledge).

- To become fit and run a marathon, you will need to spend a lot of time running. If you do not have the time or interest to devote many hours every week to running, this goal may not work for you. If you find this is the case, you could adjust your goals; there are other ways to become fit that do not involve spending hours and hours running.

- If you want to open your own independent bookstore but you have no experience running a business, have no capital (money) to put towards opening the business, and you have no knowledge about how bookstores work, or you're not really interested in reading, you may not be successful in achieving your goals.

Set priorities. At any given moment, you have a number of goals all in different states of completion. Deciding which goals are more important or time-sensitive than others is crucial. If you find yourself with too many goals, you're going to feel overwhelmed and are less likely to accomplish them.

- It may help to choose a few top priorities. This will provide you focus when conflicting goals come up. If it's a choice between completing one or two minor goals and completing one top priority, you know to choose the top priority.

- If you're working towards becoming fit and you have set the smaller goals "to eat more healthily," "to run a 5K," and "to swim 1 mile, 3 days per week," you may find that you do not have the time or energy to do all of those things at once. You can prioritize; if you want to run a marathon, first running a 5K may be more important to your goal than swimming every week. You may want to continue eating better, because that is good for your overall health in addition to helping you run.

- If you're working towards opening your own bookstore, you may need to obtain a business license and be sure you can qualify for a business loan (if you need one) before you begin selecting specific books to carry in your store.

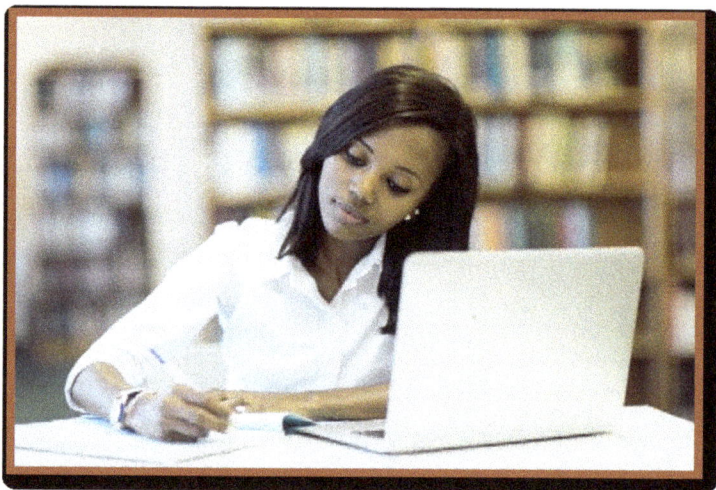

Keep track of your progress. Writing in a journal is a great way to keep track of both personal and professional progress. Checking in with yourself and acknowledging the progress made towards a certain goal is key to staying motivated. It may even encourage you to work harder.

- Asking a friend to keep you on track can help you stay focused. For example, if you're training for the big race, having a friend to regularly meet up with and work out with can keep you on track with your progress.
- If you are getting fit by working towards a marathon, keep a running journal in which you record how far you ran, how much time it took, and how you felt. As you improve more and more, it can be a great confidence boost to go back and see how far you've come since you started.
- It may be a bit more difficult to track your progress towards opening your own business, but writing down all of your goals and sub-goals, then crossing them out or indicating when each one is complete can help you track the work that you've done.

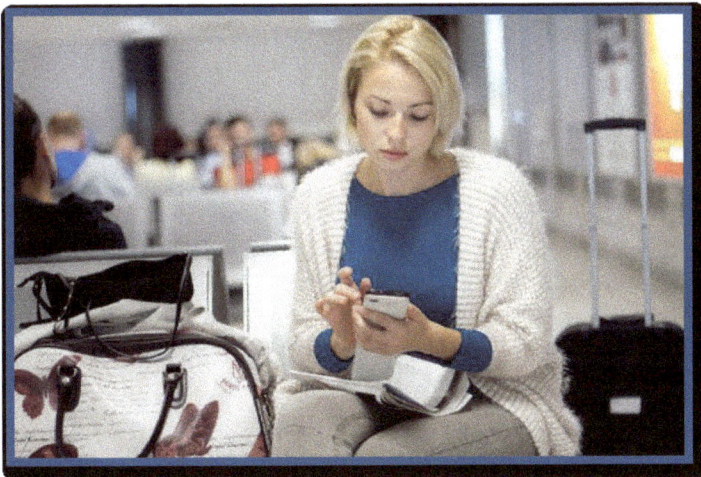

Assess your goals. Acknowledge when you have reached goals and allow yourself to celebrate accordingly. Take this time to assess the goal process—from inception to completion. Consider if you were happy with the time frame, your skill set, or if the goal was reasonable.

- For example, once you have run your first 5K, be grateful that you've completed a goal, even if it seems small one in comparison to your bigger goal of running a marathon.
- Of course, when you open the doors of your independent bookstore and you make your first sale to a customer, you'll celebrate, knowing that you have worked towards your goal successfully!

Keep setting goals. Once you have achieved goals—even major life goals—you will want to continue to grow and set new goals for yourself.

- Once you run your marathon, you should assess what you'd like to do next. Do you want to run another marathon, but improve your time? Do you want to diversify and try a triathlon or an Ironman race? Or do you want to go back to running shorter distance races—5Ks or 10Ks?
- If you have opened your independent bookstore, do you want to work on implementing community events, such as book clubs or literacy tutoring? Or do you want to make more money? Would you like to open additional locations or expand by adding a coffee shop inside or next door to your bookstore?

NOTES

_____

_____

_____

_____

_____

_____

_____

_____

_____

_____

_____

_____

_____

_____

Chapter Four

Finances

Section One – Young Adults

Section Two - Teenagers

If a person gets his attitude toward money straight, it will help straighten out almost every other area in his life.
~ Rev. Billy Graham, Evangelist

Most people fail to realize that money is both a test and trust from God.
~ Rick Warren, Minister

SECTION ONE- YOUNG ADULTS

Personal financial management is a subject that is not taught in many schools, but it is something that nearly everyone has to deal with in their lives later on. Here are some statistics: Some 58% of Americans do not have a retirement plan in place for how they will manage their finances when they get old. While people generally believe they'll need about $300,000 to support themselves in retirement, the average American has only about $25,000 saved at the time of retirement. Average household credit card debt among Americans now stands at a distressing $15,204. If these facts are alarming to you, and you want to reverse the trend, you must plan for your present and your future. Planning, as it relates to finances, means making a budget.

Part One- Make a Budget

For one month, keep track of all your expenses. You don't have to limit yourself; just get an idea of what you spend money on during any given month. Save all your receipts, make note of how much cash you need versus how much you expense to credit cards, and figure out how much money you have left over when the calendar turns.

After the first month, take stock of what you spent. Don't write down what you *wished* you had spent; write down what you *actually* spent. Categorize your purchases in a way that makes sense to you. A simple list of your monthly expenses might look something like this:

- Monthly income: $3,000
- Expenses:
    - Rent/mortgage: $800
    - Household bills (utilities/electric/cable):$125
    - Groceries: $300
    - Dining out: $125

- Gas: $100
- Emergency medical: $200
- Discretionary: $400
- Savings: $900

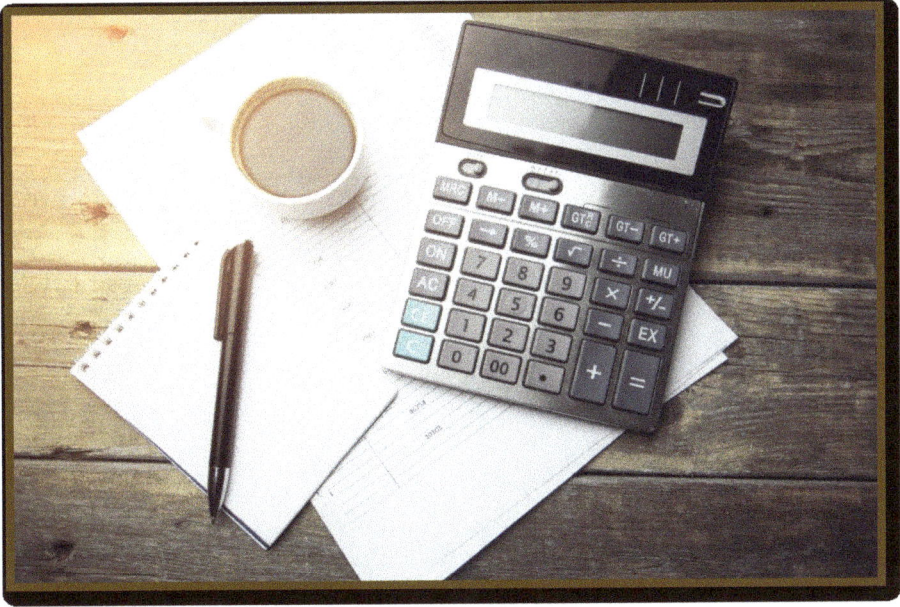

Now, write down your actual budget. Based on the month of actual expenses — and your own knowledge of your spending history — budget out how much of your income you want to allocate to each category every month.

- In your budget, make separate columns for *projected* budget and *actual* budget. Your projected budget is how much you intend to spend on a category; this should stay the same from month to month and be calculated at the beginning of the month. Your actual budget is how much you end up spending; it fluctuates from month to month and is calculated at the end of the month.

- Many people leave significant room in their budget for savings. You don't have to structure your budget to include savings, but it's generally thought of as a smart idea. Professional financial planners advise their clients to set aside at least 10% to 15% of their total earnings for savings. Savings can be used for emergencies, a special vacation, or a specific project/purchase.

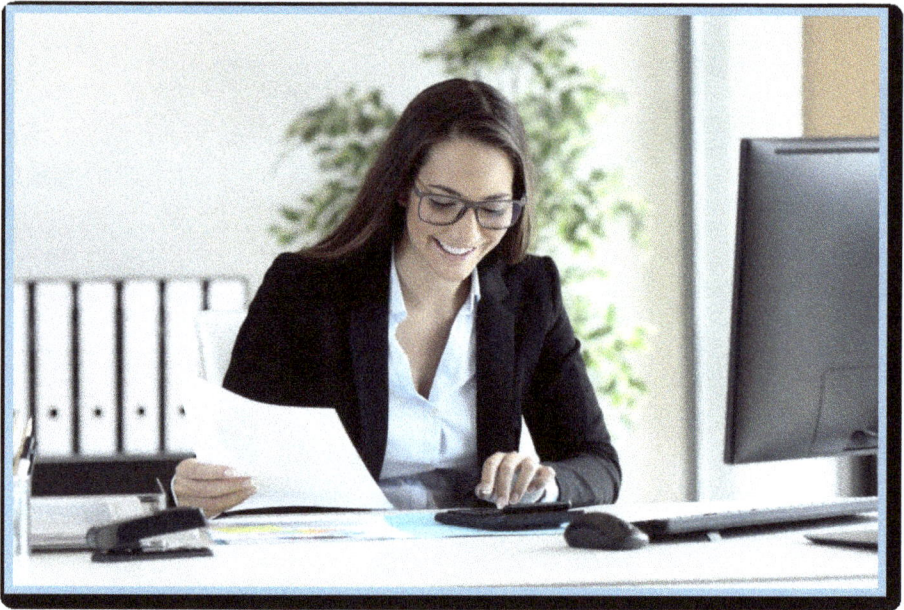

Be honest with yourself about your budget. It's your money — there's really no sense in lying to yourself about how much you're going to spend when making a budget. The only person you hurt when doing this is yourself. On the other hand, if you have no idea how you spend your money, your budget may take a few months to solidify. In the meantime, don't put down any hard numbers until you can get realistic with yourself.

- For example, if you have $500 dollars allocated to savings every month, but know that it will consistently be a stretch in order to meet that goal, don't put it down. Put down a number that's realistic. Then, go back to your budget and see if you can't tweak it to loosen up cash somewhere else, and then funnel it into your savings.

Keep track of your budget over time. The hard part of a budget is that your expenses may change from month to month. The great part of a budget is that you'll have kept track of those changes, giving you an accurate idea of where your money went during the year.

- Setting a budget will open your eyes to how much money you spend, if they haven't been opened already. Many people, after setting a budget, realize that they spend money on pretty petty things. This knowledge allows them to adjust their spending habits and put the money towards more meaningful areas.

- Plan for the unexpected. Setting a budget will also teach you that you never know when you'll have to pay for something unexpected — but that the unexpected will come to be expected. You obviously don't *plan* on your car breaking down, or your child needing medical attention, but it pays to expect these contingencies to happen, and to be prepared for them financially when they come.

Part 2- Spend Your Money Successfully

When you can borrow/rent, don't buy. How often have you bought a DVD only to have let it collect dust for years, without using it? Books, magazines, DVDs, tools, party supplies, and athletic equipment can all be rented for smaller amounts of money. Renting often saves you the hassle of upkeep, keeps room in your storage, and generally causes you to treat items better.

- Don't just rent blindly. If you use an item for long enough, it may be best to buy. Perform a simple cost analysis to see whether renting or buying is in your best interests.

If you have the money, pay a high down payment on your mortgage. For many people, buying a home is the most costly and significant payment they'll ever make in their lives. For this reason, it helps to know how to spend your mortgage money wisely. Your goal to pay off your mortgage should be to minimize interest payments and fees while balancing out the rest of your budget.

- Prepay early up front. The first five to seven years of a mortgage are generally when your interest payments are going to be the highest. If you can, take your tax return and funnel a portion of it back into your mortgage. Paying off early will help increase your equity fast by lowering your interest payments.
- See if you can't make bi-weekly payments instead of monthly payments. Instead of making 12

payments on your mortgage in a year, see if you can't make 26 payments on your mortgage instead. This will allow you to save thousands of dollars, provided there aren't any fees associated with it. Some lenders charge significant fees ($300 to $400) in order to give you the privilege, and even then they may only apply the payment once a month.

- Talk with your lender about refinancing. If you can refinance your loan down from 6.7% to 5.7%, for example, while still making the same payments, go for it. You could knock off *years* on your mortgage.

Understand that owning a credit card may be very important for establishing credit. A credit score of 750 or above may unlock significantly lower interest rates and opportunities for new loans — nothing to sneeze at. Even if you rarely use the credit card, it's important to have one. If you don't trust yourself, just lock it in a drawer.

- Treat your credit card like cash — that's what it is. Some people treat their credit cards like unlimited spending devices, running up balances they know they can't pay off and only making the minimum monthly payment. If you're going to do this, be prepared to spend significant amounts of your money on interest payments and fees.

- Shoot for a low credit utilization. A low credit utilization means that the debt you put on your credit card is proportionally low to your overall limit. In plain English, that means that if you have an average monthly balance of $200 on your credit card but your limit is $2,000, the ratio of your debt to your limit is very low, about 1:10. If you have an average monthly balance of $200 on your credit card but your limit is $400, your credit utilization is going to shoot through the roof, about 1:2.

Spend what you have, not what you hope to make. You may think of yourself as a high earner, but if your money doesn't back up that statement, you're shooting yourself in the foot acting like you are. The **first** and **greatest** rule of spending money is this: Unless it's an emergency, only spend money that you have, not money that you expect to make. This should keep you out of debt and planning well for the future. When it comes to money, be who you are and not who you hope to be. As you earn more money, you can wisely increase your spending. Until then, don't try to keep up with the Joneses.

Part 3- Make Smart Investments

Familiarize yourself with different investment options. As we grow up, we realize that the financial world out there is so much more complicated than we envisioned as children. The more you know about financial instruments and possibilities, the better off you'll be when it comes to investing your money, even if that wisdom consists only of knowing when to back away. And at the time, that may be the wisest decision you can make.

Take advantage of any retirement plans your employer offers. Often, employees can opt into a retirement 401(k) plan. In this plan, a portion of your paycheck is automatically transferred to a savings plan. This is a great way of saving, because payments come out of their paycheck before it's cut; most people never even notice the payments.

- Talk with your company's HR representative about employer matching. Some larger companies with robust benefit plans will actually match the amount of money you put into your 401(k), effectively doubling your investment. So if you choose to put in $1,000 each paycheck, your company may pay an additional $1,000, making it a $2,000 investment each paycheck.

If you're going to put money into the stock market, don't gamble with it. Many people try to day trade in the stock market, betting on small gains and losses in individual stocks every day. While this can be an effective way of making money for the seasoned individual, it's extremely risky, and more like gambling than investing. *If you want to make a safe investment in the stock market, invest for the long term.* That means leaving your money invested for 10, 20, 30 years or more.

- Look at company fundamentals (how much cash they have on hand, what their product history is, how they value their employees, and what their strategic alliances are) when choosing which stocks to invest in. You're essentially making a bet that the current stock price is undervalued and will rise in the future.

- For safer bets, look at mutual funds when buying stocks. Mutual funds are bundles of stocks collected together to minimize risk. Think about it like this: if you've invested all of your money in a single stock and the stock price plummets, you lose; if you've invested all your money equally in 100 different stocks, many stocks can completely fail without affecting your bottom line. This is basically how mutual funds mitigate risk.

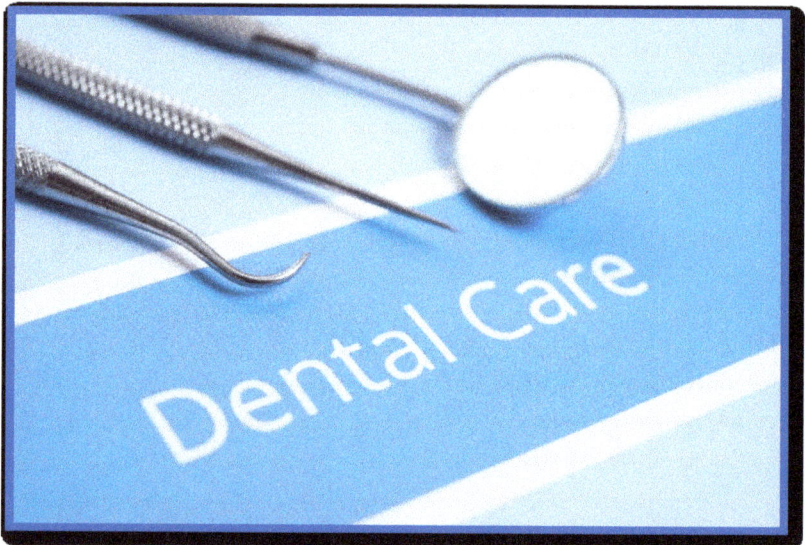

Have good insurance coverage. Smart people expect the unexpected and have a plan for what they'll do just in case. You never know when you'll need a large sum of money during an emergency. Having good insurance coverage can really help tide you over through a crisis. Talk with your family about different kinds of insurance that you can purchase to help you in the event of an emergency:

- Life insurance (if you or a spouse unexpectedly dies)
- Health insurance (if you have to pay for unexpected hospital and/or doctor bills)
- Homeowner's insurance (if something unexpected harms or destroys your home)
- Disaster insurance (for tornadoes, earthquakes, floods, fires, etc.)

Think about getting a Roth IRA for retirement. In addition to, or perhaps instead of, your traditional 401(k) plan — which is usually an employee retirement plan and a little different from employer to employer— talk with a financial advisor about getting a Roth IRA. Roth IRAs are retirement plans that let you invest a certain amount of money, and extract it, tax-free, after you turn 60. (Well, technically, 59 ½.)

- Roth IRAs are sometimes invested in securities, stocks and bonds, mutual funds, and annuities, giving them the opportunity to grow significantly over the course of many years. If you invest in an IRA early on, any compound interest you earn (interest on top of interest) can create significant increases in your investment over time.
- Consult with an insurance advisor about guaranteed income products. This type of planning allows you to receive a guaranteed amount in retirement that recurs each year without stopping as long as you shall live. This protects you from running out of money in retirement. Sometimes these payments continue for your spouse after your passing.

Part 4- Build Your Savings

Start by putting away as much of your expendable (excess) income as possible. Make savings a priority in your life.

Even if your budget is small, tweak your finances, so you save greater than 10% of your total earnings.

- Think of it like this: If you manage to save $10,000 per year — which is less than $1,000 per month — in 15 years, you'll have $150,000 plus interest. That's enough money to put a kid through college today, but not tomorrow if that child has just been born. So, start saving and you may have a significant down payment for that child or for a wonderful house.

- Start saving young. Even if you're still in school, saving is still important. People who save well treat it more as an ethic than necessity. If you save early, and then invest that savings wisely, a small initial contribution can snowball (compound) into a significant sum. It literally pays to be forward-thinking.

Start an emergency fund. Saving is all about putting away expendable income. Having expendable income means not having debt. Not having debt means being prepared for emergencies. Therefore, a rainy-day fund can really help you out when it comes to saving money.

- Think about it like this: your car breaks down and you suddenly have $2,000 in extra payments. You didn't plan on this happening, so you have to take out a loan. Credit is tightening up, so your interest rates might be pretty high. Pretty soon, you're paying 6 or 7 percent interest on a loan, which cuts into your ability to save for the next half-year.
  - If you had an emergency fund, you could have avoided bringing on the debt and the

associated interest rates, in the first place. Being prepared really pays.

When you've started saving for retirement and put money in your emergency fund, put away three to six months' worth of expenses. Again, saving is all about being prepared for the uncertainty of it all. If you're unexpectedly laid off work, or your company reduces your commission, you don't want to take on debt in order to finance your life. Setting aside three, six, or even nine months' worth of expenses will help ensure that you're in the clear, even if disaster strikes.

Begin paying off your debt once you're established. Whether it's credit card debt or debt left on your mortgage, having debt can seriously cut into your ability to save. Start with debt that has the highest interest rate. (If it's your mortgage, try paying off larger chunks of it, but focus on non-mortgage payments first.) Then, move onto your second-highest rate loan, and begin paying that off. Move down the line, in decreasing order, until you've paid off your entire debt load.

Begin really ramping up for retirement. If you're getting to be that age (45 or 50), and you haven't started saving for retirement, it's really important to start ramping up right away. Make your maximum contributions to your IRA ($5,000) and your 401(k) ($16,500) every year; if you're older than 50, you can even make so-called catch-up contributions if you want to pad your retirement savings.

- Put a high priority on saving money for retirement — even higher priority than saving for your children's college education. Whereas, you can always borrow money to help pay for college, you can't borrow money to help fund retirement.

- If you're totally in the dark about how much money you should be saving, use an online retirement-savings calculator to aid you.
- Consult a financial planner or advisor. If you want to maximize your retirement savings because you have no clue how to start, talk with a licensed professional planner. Planners are trained to invest your money wisely, and usually have a track record of return on investment (ROI). On the one hand, you'll have to pay for their services; on the other hand, you're paying them to make you money. Not a bad deal.

SECTION TWO- TEENAGERS

You may not have a full-time job or a mortgage. But basic budgeting skills can help you plan spending and set yourself up for long-term success handling money. Here are six steps to get you started.

1. Determine Your Income

The first step in building a budget is figuring out how much money comes in: regular income, such as paychecks from jobs and allowances, as well as money given to you on birthdays or holidays. Add up what you receive in a month—that's your total monthly income.

2. Calculate required expenses

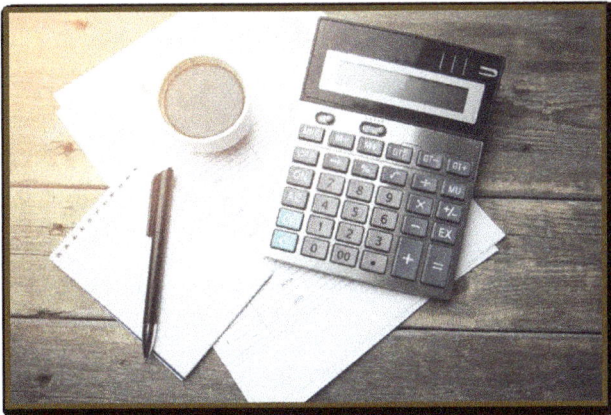

Required expenses are necessary costs you must pay regularly—they're the must-haves. For a high school student, this could be a monthly cell phone bill, or gas and car insurance if you drive. Total these costs over a month to determine a baseline set of expenses.

3. Do a little math

Once you have a total for the required expenses, subtract that number from your income. This reveals whether you have enough to cover necessities, as well as how much money is left over.

4. Talk about the fun things

Once you've covered necessary expenditures, what's left can go into your savings account. You also could use extra funds for discretionary purchases such as going to the movies or buying concert tickets—the nice-to-haves. But remember money is finite, and sometimes that means making trade-offs. For example, explain that buying an expensive piece of clothing now may mean postponing a bigger purchase.

5. Get what you want

You may not be able to afford some big-ticket items right away, such as a bicycle or even a car. In this case, your parent can help you set a savings goal and then plan how to achieve it.

6. Balance the budget

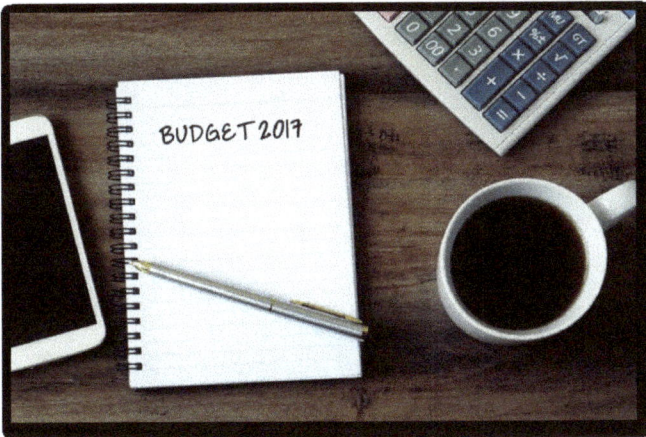

Your spending should not exceed your income. If you overspend, you should look for ways to cut back spending or increase income.

For example, you may decide to carpool one month to save on gas and use the extra funds to buy a concert ticket. You can boost income by taking on extra jobs, perhaps mowing a neighbor's lawn or babysitting.

Learning to budget while you are young will make you a more financially responsible adult and be able to enjoy more in life sooner rather than later.

NOTES

_____

_____

_____

_____

_____

_____

_____

_____

_____

_____

_____

_____

Chapter Five

Relationships

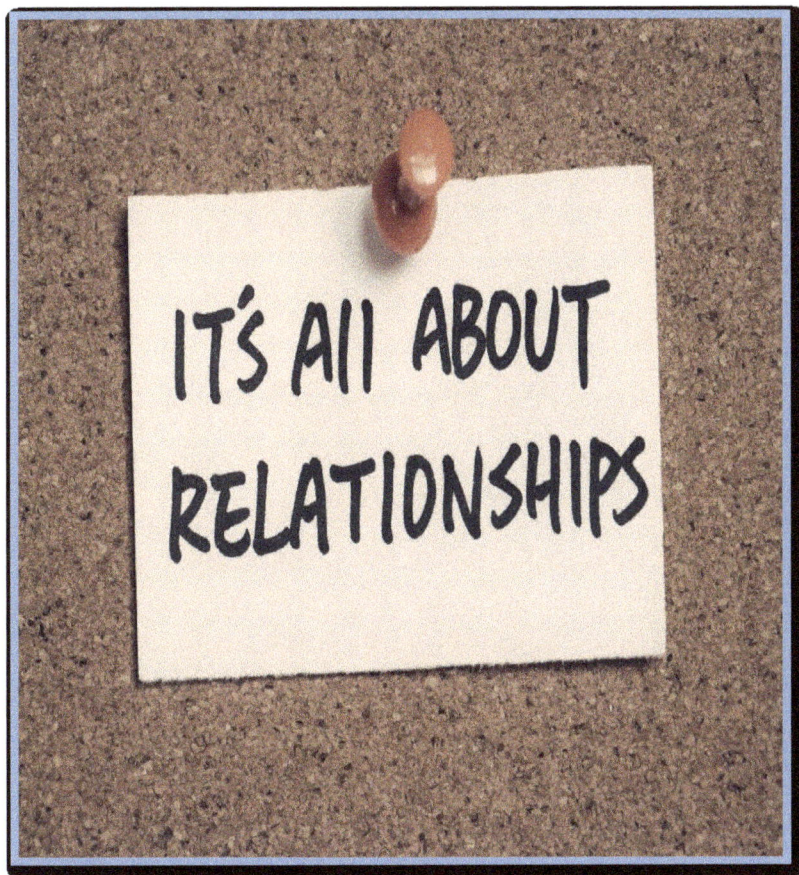

Desired Love

A soft touch and gentle kiss
Breathe in me and send me into bliss
Show me real love without touching me
Touch me without damaging me
Am I precious to you?
More than rubies
Am I desired love
Will you let GOD lead you to me
Or will you come when I call
Tell me am I desired love

© Sabrina P. Foster

The Greeks had four words to describe what we call love: Eros (romantic love), Phileo (enjoyment, fondness, friendship), Storge (family loyalty) and Agape (unconditional love with stick-ability). I like to think of them broadly as

1. **Eros**- A love felt particularly within the body (trembling excitement, elation, joy), coloured and underpinned by deep and beautiful procreative urges. C.S. Lewis distinguishes Eros from natural sexual urges and lusts, because Eros is a state of the heart, and while it is intimately related to sex, sex can exist, and often does exist, without Eros enlivening it. It leads to children, family, joy and laughter. It is good and right, but it is usually not enough to sustain a relationship long term. Eros is an exulted and beautifully idealistic love, usually between a man and woman, but can also be "platonic" and extend to deeply intimate friendships.

2. **Phileo**- If Eros is the love of the body, Phileo is the love of the soul. It is easy love and affection; it is bent towards our natural tastes and preferences. It embodies culture and beliefs. It's about the friendship you feel towards people like you, with the same interests, social graces, and style. In the scriptures, this kind of friendship love is used to describe many relationships.

God is said to have this kind of love for us and Jesus. Jesus felt this kind of love for His disciples; parents felt it about their children and children to their parents. It is not then a shallow love, but rich in emotion and feeling, like when your heart beams towards your children when they do something wonderful. However, it is also described as a negative shallow love, natural and exclusive and con- ditional. Phileo is soul love, and it's strength and value will depend on the elevation of the soul of the bearer.

3. Agape- Is more of a parental, mature, sacrificial kind of love. The Thayer Lexicon describes agape beautifully

when it says "to take pleasure in the thing, prize it above all other things, be unwilling to abandon it or do without it." In a way it is as idealistic as Eros, in that it is a crazy love that will not let go.

Agape loves, usually at cost to the bearer. Agape puts the beloved first and sacrifices pride, self-interest and possessions for the sake of that beloved. This is the love that God has for us which inspired Him to sacrifice His son and for His son to obey and sacrifice Himself. It is the kind of love we are commanded to have for one another. It is a love of supreme greatness.

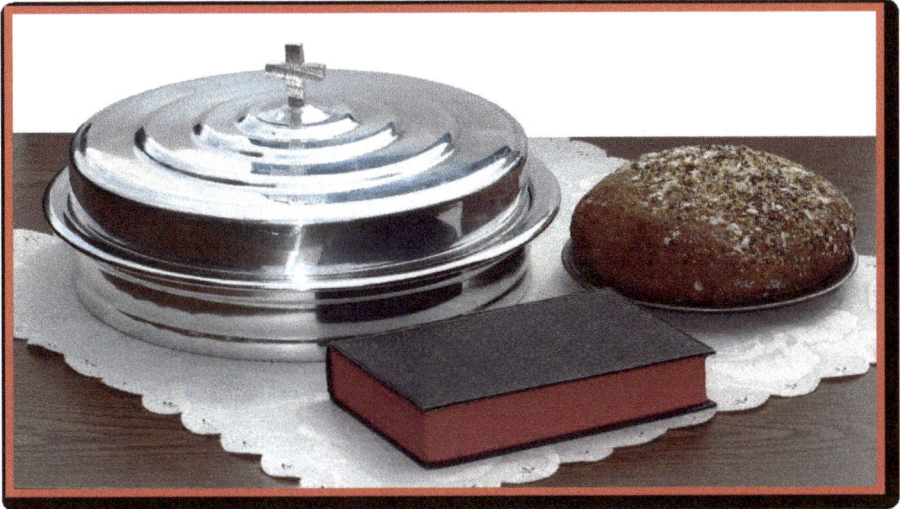

4. **Storge**- This is the love of community and family. Often dutiful, sometimes unfeeling, but very strong nonetheless. It is a natural, carnal love, but powerful enough to be a real hindrance to spiritual growth, especially when family and culture are holding you down. It is a love that may pull you towards a lesser path.

Obviously, all of these loves work together, but only Agape is free from the error of our humanity. Agape is the glue that holds the other loves fast and gives us the wisdom and patience when the other loves fail. If we make it our goal to always be forgiving and merciful and believe in doing good to all men, and then do it, the other loves will stand, and your life will be full of the rich blessings of Phileo friendships and intimacies of the sweetest and loveliest kind.

You will stand up in the midst of your family and people and call them back to walk on pleasanter paths and on smoother highways. So, seek first the high love Agape, a love that sacrifices, forgives and believes, the love of Christ, freely given to those who ask and receive. Drink deeply of Christ's love for you, for the father's love for you, of this eternal and perfect love, and all these other loves will be added unto you.

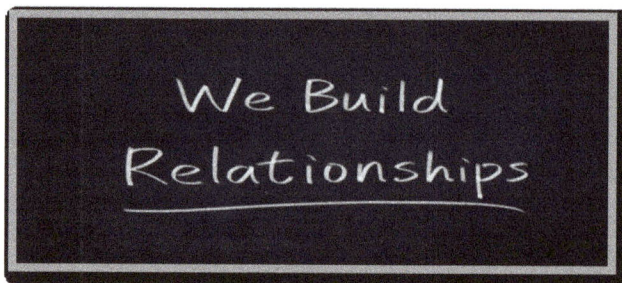

We Build
Relationships

NOTES

_____

_____

_____

_____

_____

_____

_____

_____

_____

_____

_____

_____

_____

_____

Chapter 6

Keeping a Healthy Mind
(Mental Wellness)

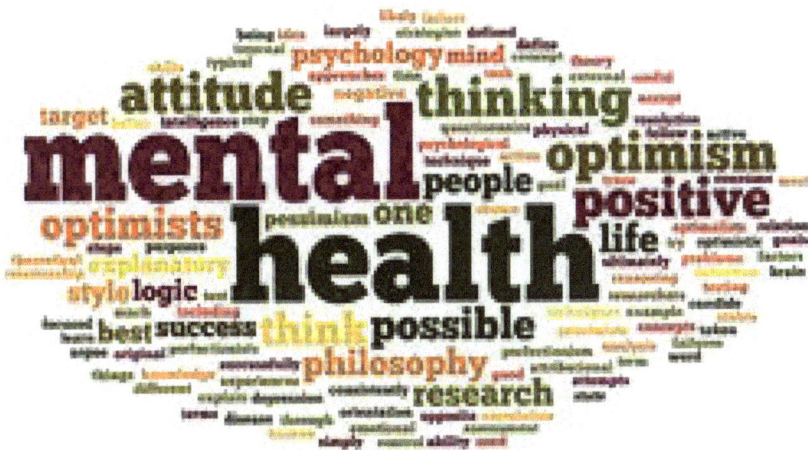

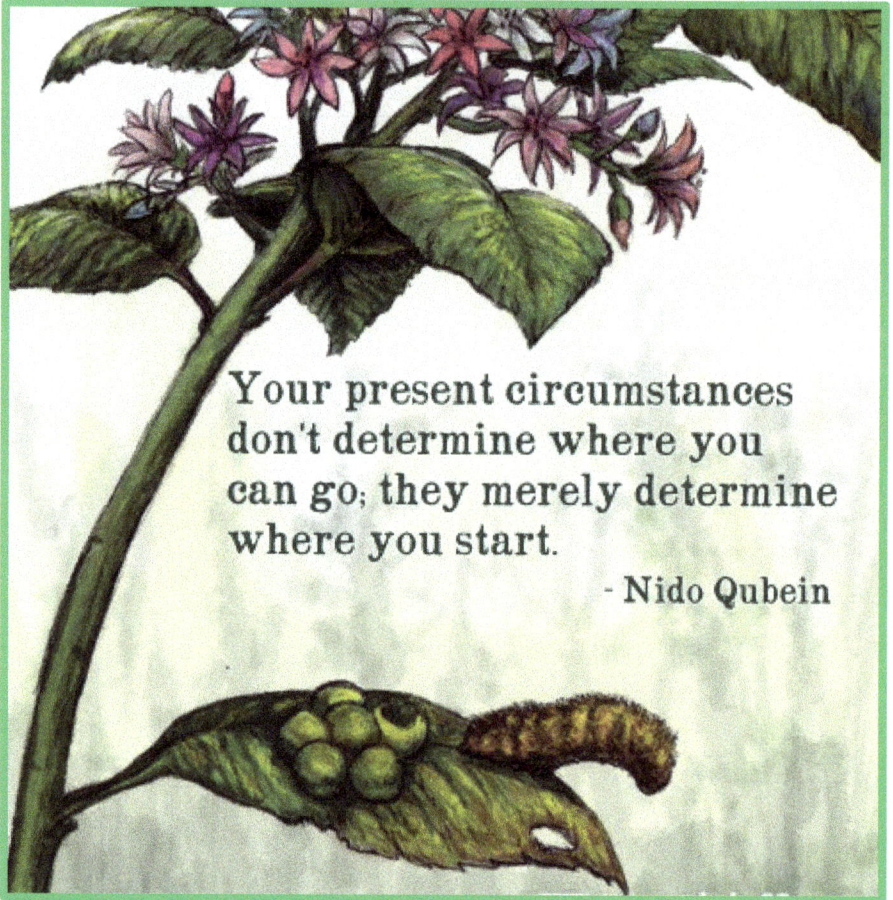

Your present circumstances don't determine where you can go; they merely determine where you start.

- Nido Qubein

People have a tendency to focus most, if not all, their attention on their financial and physical health. They balance their checking accounts and work out at the gym on a weekly basis. And, there is absolutely no fault in taking care of one's finances and physical well-being. However, if we do not give the same time and attention to the stability of our mental health, our finances and our body's condition will not matter.

This chapter focuses your attention on how you can be mentally well- regardless of the conditions with which you may face.

1. Talk about your feelings

Talking about your feelings can help you stay in good mental health and deal with times when you feel troubled. Talking about your feelings isn't a sign of weakness; it's part of taking charge of your wellbeing and doing what you can to stay healthy. Talking can be a way to cope with a problem you've been carrying around in your head for a while. Feeling listened to can help you feel more supported.

And it works both ways. If you open up, it might encourage others to do the same. It's not always easy to describe how you're feeling. If you can't think of one word, use several. How does it feel inside your head? What does it make you feel like doing? You don't need to sit your loved ones down for a big conversation about your wellbeing. Many people feel more comfortable when these conversations develop naturally – maybe when you're doing some-thing together. If it feels awkward at first, give it time. Make talking about your feelings something that you do, rather than something you avoid doing.

2. Keep active

Regular exercise can boost your self-esteem and can help you concentrate, sleep, and look and feel better. Exercise keeps the brain and your other vital organs healthy and is also a significant benefit towards improving your mental health.

Exercising doesn't just mean doing sport or going to the gym. Walks in the park, gardening or housework can also keep you active. Experts say that most people should do about 30 minutes of exercise at least five days a week. Try to make physical activity that you enjoy a part of your day.

3. Eat well

What we eat may affect how we feel. For example, caffeine and sugar can have an immediate effect. But food can also have a long-lasting effect on your mental health. Your brain needs a mix of nutrients in order to stay healthy and function well, just like the other organs in your body. A diet that's good for your physical health is also good for your mental health. A healthy, balanced diet includes:

• Lots of different types of fruit and vegetables
• Wholegrain cereals or bread
• Nuts and seeds
• Dairy products
• Oily fish
• Plenty of water

Three meals a day or five smaller snacks throughout the day, plus plenty of water, is ideal for maintaining good mental health. Try to limit how many high caffeine, sugary drinks or how much alcohol you have.

4. Drink sensibly

We often drink alcohol to change our mood. Some people drink to deal with fear or loneliness, but the effect is only temporary. When the drink wears off, you feel worse because of the way the alcohol has affected your brain and the rest of your body. Drinking is not a good way to manage difficult feelings. Apart from the damage that too much alcohol can do to your body, you would need more and more alcohol each time to feel the same. This is called building 'tolerance' to the substance. Occasional light drinking is perfectly healthy and enjoyable for most people. Stay within the recommended daily alcohol limits:

• Three to four units a day for men
• Two to three units a day for women

Many people smoke or use drugs or other substances to change how they feel. But, again, the effects are short-lived. Just like alcohol, the more you use, the more you crave. Nicotine and drugs don't deal with the causes of difficult feelings. They don't solve problems. Therefore, you should avoid addictive substances.

5. **Keep in touch**

Strong family ties and supportive friends can help you deal with the stresses of life. Friends and family can make you feel included and cared for. They can offer different views from whatever's going on inside your own head. They can help keep you active, keep you grounded and can help you solve practical problems. There's nothing better than catching up with someone face to face, but that's not always possible. You can also give them a call, drop them a note, or chat with them online instead.

Keep the lines of communication open: It's good for you! If you're feeling out of touch with some people, look back at the section on talking about your feelings and get started! It's worth working at relationships that make you feel loved or valued. But, if you think being around someone is damaging your mental health, it may be best to take a break from that person, or call it a day completely. It's possible to end a relationship in a way that feels okay for both of you. It can be hard to cope when someone close to you dies or if you lose him/her in another way. Counseling for bereavement or loss can help you explore your feelings. The next section suggests how to find a counselor.

6. Ask for help

None of us are superhuman. We all sometimes get tired or overwhelmed by how we feel or when things don't go to plan. If things are getting too much for you and you feel you can't cope, ask for help. Your family or friends may be able to offer practical help or a listening ear.

Local services are there to help you. For example, you could:

• Join a support group, like Alcoholics Anonymous or Narcotics Anonymous, to help you make changes to your life.

You can also consider getting help from your general practitioner if difficult feelings are:

• Stopping you from getting on with life
• Having a big impact on the people you live or work with
• Affecting your mood over several weeks

Over a third of visits to general practitioners are about mental health. Your general practitioner may suggest ways that you or your family can help you, or they may refer you to a specialist or another part of the health service.

7. Take a break

A change of scene or a change of pace is good for your mental health. It could be a five-minute pause from cleaning your kitchen, a half-hour lunch break at work, or a weekend exploring somewhere new. A few minutes can be enough to de-stress you. Give yourself some 'me time'.

Taking a break may mean being very active. It may mean not doing very much at all. Take a deep breath… and relax. Try putting your feet up. Listen to your body. If you're really tired, give yourself time to sleep. Without good sleep, our mental health suffers and our concentration goes downhill. Sometimes, the world can wait.

8. Do something you're good at

What do you love doing? What activities can you lose yourself in? What did you love doing in the past? Enjoying yourself can help beat stress. Doing an activity you enjoy probably means you're good at it, and achieving something boosts your self-esteem. Concentrating on a hobby, like gardening or doing crosswords, can help you forget your worries for a while and can change your mood. It can be good to have an interest where you're not seen as someone's mom or dad, partner or employee. You're just you. An hour of sketching lets you express yourself creatively. A morning on the football pitch gets you active and gives you the chance to meet new people.

9. Accept who you are

Some of us make people laugh, some are good at math, and others cook fantastic meals. Some of us share our lifestyle with the people who live close to us, others live very differently. We're all different. It's much healthier to accept that you're unique than to wish you were more like someone else. Feeling good about yourself boosts your confidence to learn new skills, visit new places, and make new friends. Good self-esteem helps you cope when life takes a difficult turn.

Be proud of who you are. Recognize and accept the things you may not be good at, but also focus on what you can do well. If there's anything about yourself you would like to change, are your expectations realistic? If they are, work towards the change in small steps.

10. Care for others

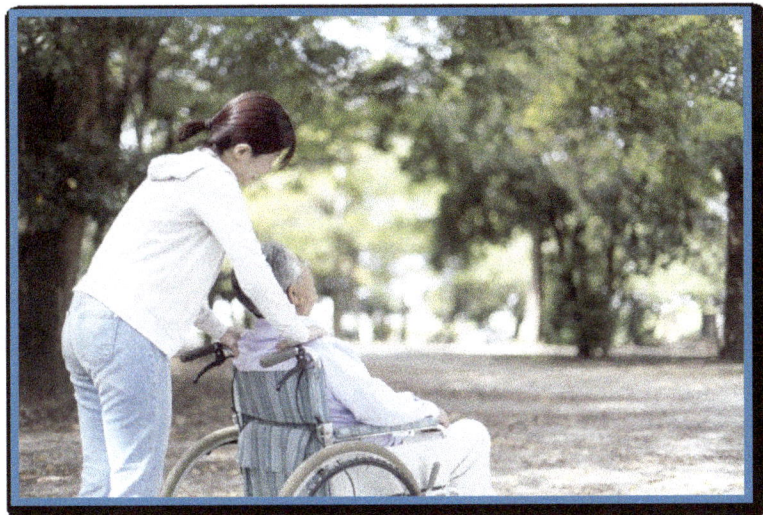

Caring for others is often an important part of keeping up relationships with people close to you. It can even bring you closer together. Why not share your skills more widely by volunteering for a local charity? Helping out can make us feel needed and valued, and that boosts our self-esteem. It also helps us to see the world from another angle. This can help to put our own problems in perspective.

Caring for a pet can improve your wellbeing too. The bond between you and your pet can be as strong as between people. Looking after a pet can bring structure to your day and can act as a link to other people. For example, some people make friends by chatting to fellow dog walkers.

NOTES

Gift of Salvation
for Non-Believers

*"For all have sinned, and come short of the
glory of God."*
(Romans 3:23)

This section was written especially for non-believers, those who have not accepted the gift of salvation. The gift of salvation saves souls from eternal damnation and is a free gift offered by God himself.

John 3:16-18 says, *"For God so loved the world, that he gave his only begotten Son, that whosoever believeth in him should not perish, but have everlasting life. For God sent not his Son into the world to condemn the world; but that the world through him might be saved. He that believeth on him is not condemned: but he that believeth not is condemned already, because he hath not believed in the name of the only begotten Son of God."*

This section of scripture tells us God's purpose for giving His son Jesus to the world. The world was in a bad condition. The world was overwrought with sin; the people were living for fleshly desires rather than for God's desires.

As a result of the world's conditions, God decided He would offer the perfect sacrifice that would save the world from being a place where people were lost and had no hope. He decided that His own son could stand in proxy for the sin-filled world, taking all sin upon Himself.

So Jesus came, born of a virgin, to save this dying world. He walked on this earth for 33 ½ years, doing the work of His Heavenly Father. At the appointed time, He died by way of crucifixion upon a cross at Calvary, on Golgatha's hill. He shed his blood and died for you and for me. Because His blood was pure, it paid the penalty for all unrighteousness and gave those who believe in Him direct access to His father's throne.

Scripture tells us in Matthew 27:51 that the veil of the temple was ripped in two from top to bottom, at the moment that Jesus' spirit left His body. As a result of the veil's removal, we are no longer required to have a high priest make intercession for us. We, as the children of the Most High God, are able to approach the throne God for ourselves, and Jesus sits on the right hand of the Father making intercession for us.

But what is even more miraculous than God offering His own son as the perfect sacrifice was the fact that when Jesus was placed in grave clothes and placed in a tomb, He only remained there until the third day. God would not have it that His son would remain in the heart of the earth forever. In order for people to believe in the awesome power of God and His dear son Jesus, a miracle had to be performed. So, on the third day, after Jesus died on the cross, He was resurrected, demonstrating the omnipotence of God. This very act was the act that would cause people to believe in a god that reigns supreme and holds the power of the universe in His very hands, a god that could save them from themselves.

Today, if you are an unbeliever, you can change your destiny. You can change where you will spend your eternity. Our Heavenly Father gives us the freedom of choice about how we want to live our life here on earth and how we want to spend eternity. In Deuteronomy 30:19, God boldly declares, *"I call heaven and earth to record this day against you, that I have set before you life and death, blessing and cursing: therefore choose life, that both thou and thy seed may live."*

So, dear friend what choice will you make today? Will you spend your eternity with the Creator or will you suffer Hell's eternal flames? Again, the choice is yours. Just as the men aboard the ship who were with Jonah became believers, you too can make a choice to accept the only one and true living God as your god.

If after reading the above passages, you have decided that you want to spend your eternity in Heaven with God, the creator, and His son Jesus, and the Holy Spirit, read through what has affectionately come to be known as the Roman's Road. This is the road to salvation. As you read through the scriptures that comprise the Roman's Road, you will also read the explanation for each scripture so you will have clarity about what you are reading and confessing.

The Roman's Road to Salvation

The road to salvation begins with Romans 3:23 which declares, *"For all have sinned, and come short of the glory of God."* This scripture explains that everyone has come short of God's glory and needs redemption. Then Romans 6:23a states, *"For the wages of sin is death."* Here, we learn that the consequence of living a life of sin is death. Everyone will experience physical death as a result of the sin committed in the garden of Eden, but those who commit themselves to a life of sin will suffer eternal damnation in the lake of fire (Rev. 19).

Continue with the rest of verse 6:23 that says, *"but the gift of God is eternal life through Jesus Christ our Lord."* There is an alternative to suffering eternal damnation. We can accept the gift of salvation by accepting Jesus as our personal lord and savior. Then, Romans 5:8 says, *"But God commendeth his love toward us, in that, while we were yet sinners, Christ died for us."* We are able to receive the gift of salvation because Christ came to earth and shed His blood for us on the cross.

Continue to Romans 10: 9-10 which says, *"That if thou shalt confess with thy mouth the Lord Jesus, and shalt believe in thine heart that God hath raised him from the dead, thou shalt be saved. For with the heart man believeth unto righteousness; and with the mouth confession is made unto salvation."* If we confess with our mouths that Jesus is the son of God, that he came and died for our sins, and that God raised Him from the dead, we will receive salvation.

Finish with Romans 10:13, which states, *"For whosoever shall call upon the name of the Lord shall be saved."* Call upon the name of God by saying these words, **"Lord Jesus, come into my heart and save me Lord. I believe that you are the Son of God who came and died on the cross for my sins. I believe that you rose from the grave. I also believe that you now sit in heaven on the right side of the Father, making intersession for me. I accept you as my Lord and my Savior."**

Now that you have confessed with your mouth that Jesus is the son of God and that He died for our sins and rose from the grave, **YOU ARE NOW SAVED!!!!** You will spend your eternity in heaven.

The next step is very important- you must find a Bible-based church that teaches the word of God and confesses the Lord Jesus Christ to be the son of God. Don't delay. Do this immediately. Do not leave yourself open to the enemy. Get connected with the saints of the Most High God and keep yourself covered with the unspotted blood of the lamb.

Here is my prayer for you.

Father God,

I thank you for the opportunity to minister your word to the unsaved, the unchurched, and the uncommitted. Father God, I pray now for the souls who have just received the gift of salvation. Lord Father, they have opened their hearts to you, and I know that you have received them into your kingdom and written their names in the Book of Life. Father God, I pray that you will touch their lives and show yourself mightily before them. Let their eyes be opened by the scales falling off, allowing them to see clearly.

Father God, I even pray for the backslider, those who have turned away from you after receiving the gift of salvation. You said in your word that you desire that none would perish. So Lord, I send your word to them right now praying that they would confess the iniquity in their heart, repent, and turn from their evil ways, so that they may receive a life of abundance. You said in your word in Matthew Chapter 14, that every knee shall bow before you and every tongue will confess that Jesus is Lord.

Father God, I pray now that we all come under subjection to your word and that we will humbly submit our lives to you. I ask all these things in the name of my Lord and Savior Jesus Christ.

Amen, Amen, Amen!!!!

I will continue to pray for your success in your walk with God. Remember, this spiritual walk that you are about to embark on will not be an easy walk, but remember, the race is not given to the swift but to those who endure to the end.

Be blessed with heaven's best. I love you!

References

Edberg, Henrik. (2017). *How to Improve Your Self-Esteem: 12 Powerful Tips.*

Office on Women's Health. (2017). girlshealth.gov

Setting Goals
http://www.wikihow.com/Set-
Goals#Practicing_Effective_Goal_Strategies_sub

About the Author

Dr. Cassundra White-Elliott resides in California with her family, where as an English/Education professor she works for various community colleges and universities.

When writing, she writes with the direction of the Holy Spirit, in an effort to share with God's people all that He has for them.

In addition to teaching and writing, Dr. White-Elliott also serves as an evangelistic teacher. She is also the founder of International Women's Commission, a ministry that serves the needs of the entire person, by attending to healing the mind, body, soul, and spirit.

Dr. White-Elliott holds a Ph.D. in Education, a Master's in English Composition, and a Bachelor's in Education.

Dr. White-Elliott is also the founder of CLF Publishing, LLC. For your publishing needs, go online to www.clfpublishing.org.

OTHER BOOKS BY THE AUTHOR

(All books can be purchased at
www.creativemindsbookstore.com)

From Despair, through Determination, to Victory!

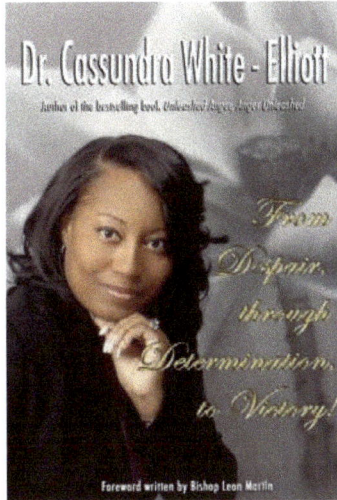

A lot can happen during a span of 40 years. The life of Dr. Cassundra White-Elliott has been anything but uneventful. From a fun-loving childhood sprinkled with incidents of abuse to a tumultuous young adulthood to a stable, secure adult life, she has experienced a full life, with much more to come. Her story is inspiring and motivating.

If anyone lacks hope, reading Dr. White-Elliott's autobiography will propel him/her into an attitude of "Maybe I can." This attitude, if nurtured and developed, will grow into an attitude of "Yes, I can." Throughout her life, Cassundra has always held in her heart the belief that she could achieve anything that she had a made-up mind to embark upon. She was determined to achieve her heart's desires, doing what God has called her to do. She takes no credit for herself. All the glory goes to God, for He is her driving force. In Him, she lives, moves, and has her being.

Through the Storm

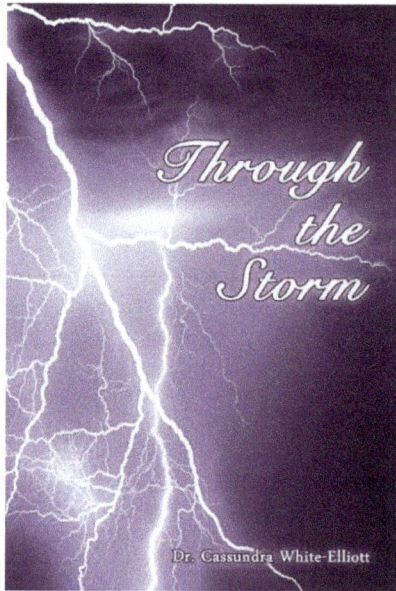

Through the Storm was duly inspired by the avaricious cloud of depression that decided to hover overhead of my daily existence in the latter part of 2007. Although I found it extremely difficult, I was once again compelled to not be defeated by just another snare that the enemy, the trickster, set for me. Once again, or more appropriately I should say *continuously*, he has exerted pernicious efforts to snatch the very life out of me by causing me to wallow in despair and to believe that I had been overcome by failure when in actuality and all reality, I was just experiencing a temporary setback. During those cloudy days, I had to remind myself daily that even though I was a target of the enemy, I am and will always be a child of the Most High god, Jehovah, who is my rock, my stability.

Unleashed Anger, Anger Unleashed

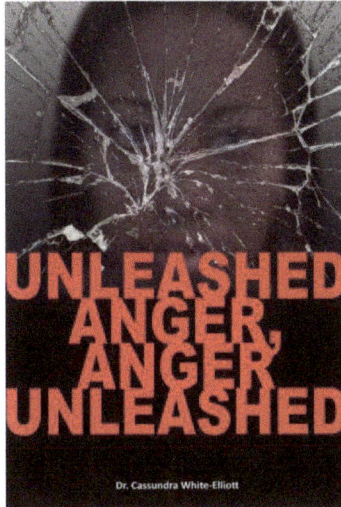

Introduction
What Is This Book All About?

As I prepared to embark upon the adventure of writing this book, I had to prepare myself to also be transparent. I have found that being transparent is required in order for healing to transpire, healing for all those that peruse the pages of this book and myself. And I may as well tell you that today, at the onset of this project, I have not been totally delivered from my condition of being an anger-filled person. However, I am definitely a work in progress. I have made strides with the assistance of my Lord and Savior, Jesus Christ, who is the head of my life. Without his love, guidance, and teachings, I would not be the woman of God I am today. I shudder to think where I could be instead and will therefore not entertain the thought.

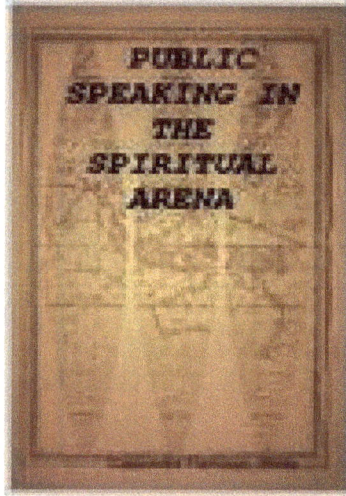

Chapter Two
How Communication Works

Purpose: This chapter will explain the six primary components of communication, identifying their purpose and how they work together.

The Source

In oral communication, the source of information is the speaker. In a church setting, the foundation of the message is God's word, but it is a speaker's interpretation of God's word that is delivered to the audience. As speakers vary, the information may vary but should have a similar essence because the foundational text is the same.

The Message

The message is the collective set of ideas that the speaker (the source) wants to deliver and/or illustrate to the audience. The message can be informative where the speaker informs the audience about a specific set of information. Or, the message may be persuasive in nature if the speaker wants to persuade the audience about conducting themselves in a specific manner, accepting God's commandments, or any number of things.

Where is Your Joppa?

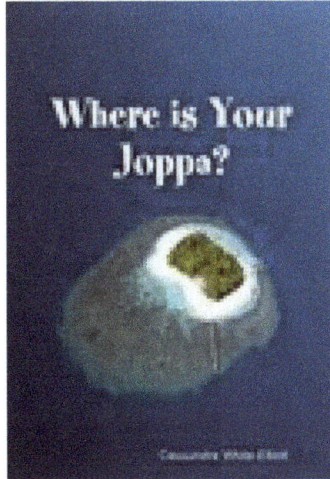

Introduction

Where is Your Joppa? was written for the express purpose of illustrating God's call for obedience in the lives of believers with respect to the individual call that He has on each of our lives. As you read throughout the various chapters, notice that the emphasis is placed on our persistent disobedience in answering God's call in a specific area of our lives. We have become a people who are similar to the Israelites when they found themselves in the middle of the wilderness, following their exodus from Egypt. Before God, they murmured and complained about their current life conditions and failed to be obedient to God's statutes delivered through His servant Moses. Their persistent disobedience caused them to lose the opportunity to see and enter the Promised Land. I ask you, "What has your disobedience cost you?" "Was your disobedience worth what it cost you?" "Do you think about the souls you could have ushered into the kingdom of God?" These are some of the questions that I pray will be answered through your reading of the book.

Mayhem in the Hamptons

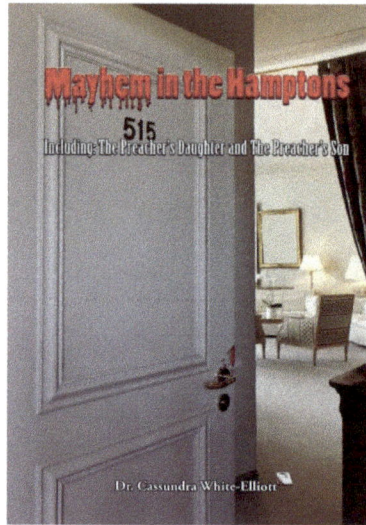

Romero and Yolanda optimistically plan for the day that is going to change their lives from being single persons to a couple who is united in holy matrimony. They, along with their parents, close friends and family, fly over to the infamous Hamptons, where only the rich and famous vacation, to have their dream wedding at the five-star Hampton Suites located on a peninsula in the Hamptons. Little do they know that their perfect day will turn out to be less than perfect when their wedding planner Mariesha Coleman suddenly goes missing!

A time when the newlyweds' lives should be filled with joy and the creation of wonderful memories, they are stricken with grief as they desperately try to find clues to help solve Mariesha's disappearance.

Mayhem in the Hamptons is a tale that shares how the horrors of a woman's past can come back to haunt her in more than one way and the impact it can have on anyone who gets in the way.

Preacher's Daughter

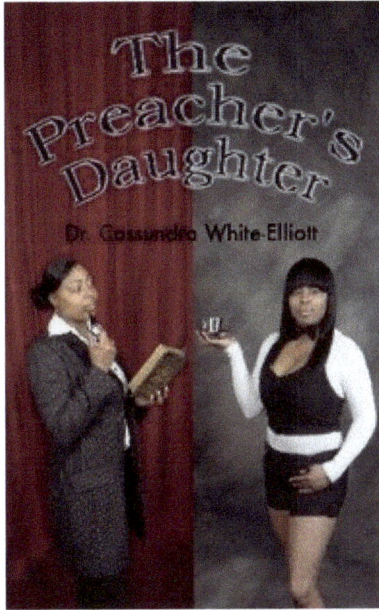

Tinisha, the daughter of a preacher, is a twenty-six year old God-fearing young woman endeavoring to complete law school so that she can make her mark in the courtroom. Working in one of the late-night clubs in Hollywood to earn money to pay her own way through school, Tinisha soon learns that life doesn't always go as planned. Finding her strength in her faith, Tinisha constantly finds herself praying as she watches God move miraculously in her life.

Preacher's Son

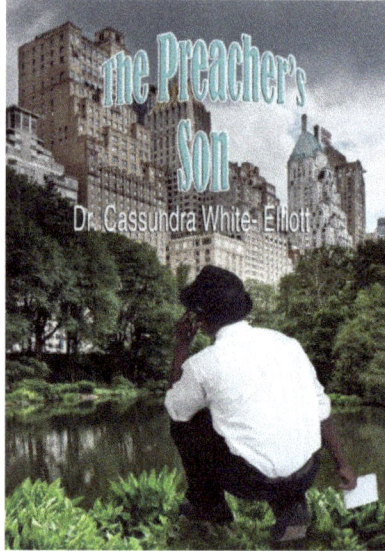

Romero Turner is a private investigator with a promising future. As he continues to build his career, he is excited about the cases he undertakes. However, his father Pastor Theodore Turner has other plans for his son's life. In the midst of trying to save his client's husband from Sylvester Domingo, a ruthless crime lord, Romero must try to salvage his relationship with his father. He must decide if ministry or life as a detective is in his future.

Lord, Teach Me to be a Blessing!

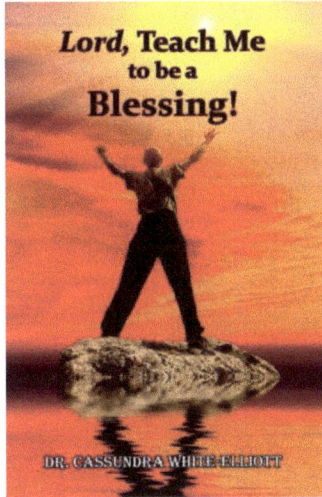

Lord, Teach Me to be a Blessing! will change a person's mentality from being centered around "me, myself, and I" to focusing on "others."

The world system teaches us that it is acceptable to place ourselves above others in an attempt to get ahead and even to survive. Herbert Spencer coined the phrase '*survival of the fittest*' after reading Charles Darwin's theory of evolution. This concept of surpassing and outdoing others is the world's philosophy.

However, the word of God does not subscribe to or promote this self-centered ideology, and therefore, neither should believers. We must hold fast to the truths outlined in Holy Scripture: "*Love thy neighbor as you love thyself*" (James 2:8) and "*It is more blessed to give than to receive*" (Acts 20:35).

While holding God's truths to be self-evident, we must demonstrate them to others, thereby showing them the way of the Lord of how to be a blessing to someone *rather* than looking to receive a blessing.

This is the very purpose of this book: to change the mentality of the world from being *self*-centered to *other* centered.

After the Dust Settles

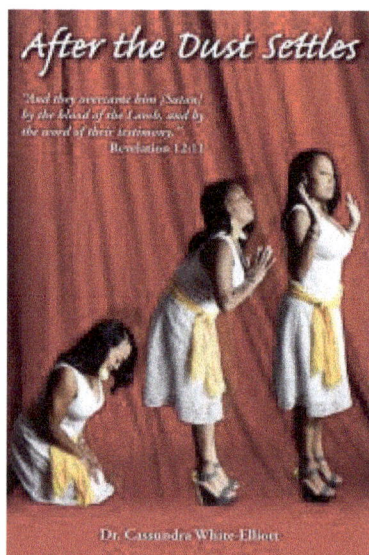

Throughout the journey of life, we all experience ups and downs and joys and pains. Most of us successfully find solutions to the situations/problems we encounter, but we often avoid dealing with the attached emotions. If we continue to ignore the emotions of pain, hurt, disappointment, anger, etc., we set ourselves up for destruction. Our families, our cultures, and our society tell us to be strong, to keep our chin up, and to grin and bear it. However, these methods of avoidance can lead us to strokes due to the undue amount of pressure we place on ourselves and/or mental illness from being unable to cope with the emotional baggage we have accumulated.

In *After the Dust Settles,* Dr. C. White-Elliott shares several situations that we all may encounter at one time or another in our lifetime and how to successfully navigate through them, so we can find ourselves emotionally healthy after the dust has settled and the situation has been rectified.

Begin reading today and experience a better tomorrow!

A Diamond in the Rough

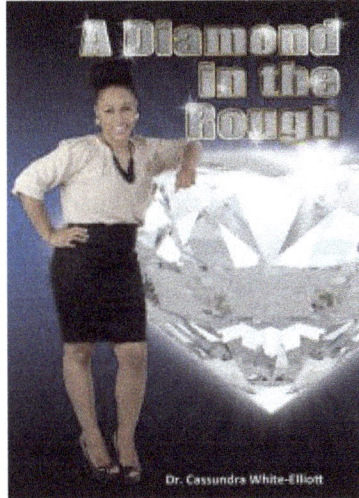

A Diamond in the Rough Architecture Firm was built and is owned and operated by lead architect Kyra Fraser. For the last five years, Kyra has been extremely successful in business, but her love life leaves much to be desired.

Kyra has set high standards for herself and does not wish to take a man in any condition and attempt to make him over. She is looking for someone who is drama free, well educated, very cultured, fun-loving, good looking, self-motivated, and the list goes on.

Will Kyra find the man of her dreams, or will her dream just continue to be a dream?

As you delve into this page-turning novel, Kyra's reality will unfold as you are drawn into her world of design, love and office drama- which includes her best friend's husband who is looking for love in all the wrong places.

365 Days of Encouragement

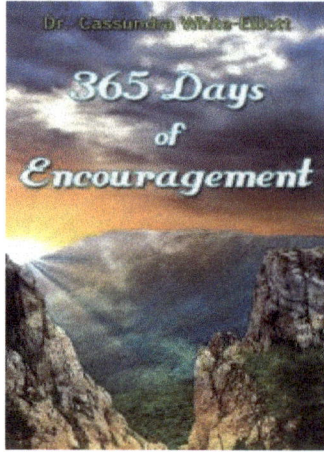

Just as our brain requires oxygen obtained from the air we breathe to sustain our mortal bodies, our spirit requires revitalization and encouragement in order to be strengthened each and every day of our lives. The revitalization and encouragement needed for the spirit of man comes directly from the word of God and assists us in walking according to the way of our heavenly Father. 365 Days of Encouragement provides a scripture a day for each day of the year. Along with the daily scripture is a brief note of commentary also for the benefit of edifying the saints of God.

It is my prayer that the people of God would live a fulfilled life through Christ Jesus. Knowing His word and understanding we can walk in the fulfillment thereof is empowering. We are instructed in II Timothy 2:15, "Study to shew thyself approved unto God, a workman that needeth not to be ashamed, rightly dividing the word of truth" (KJV). Take an opportunity to delve further into the word of God, to know His statutes and to allow your own personal life to be edified, so you can be equipped to bring glory to God and lived a fulfilled life.

A Mother's Heart

Dr. Cassundra White-Elliott

A Mother's Heart shares the unconditional love of mothers through a compilation of testimonies. Each testimony serves as a tribute to a special mother. The children of the represented mothers have lovingly written about their childhood, young adult life and/or older adult experiences they shared with their mother. As you read the writers' reflections, you will feel the expressions of love exude from the pages.

The purpose of this book is two-fold. First, it honors those mothers who stood by their children through the trials of life and showered them with unconditional love. Second, the book is a source of encouragement for mothers who may feel inadequate and question whether or not they are actually suited for motherhood. Our advice to mothers is, "Be encouraged; the journey of motherhood may seem daunting at times and you may shed some tears, but your children will never forget the love you have shown them and instilled in them to share with others."

Mothers may not be perfect, but they are definitely unmatched by any other category of person on God's green earth!

Broken Chains

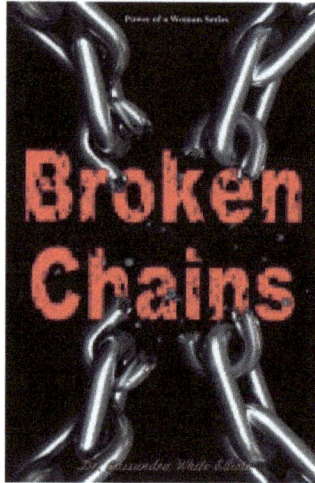

Broken Chains is an in-depth survey of five life-changing tragedies that can and will serve as chains to bind us if we are not watchful and mindful of their potential effects. In our lifetimes, we may all experience death of loved ones, sexual abuse, broken relationships, promiscuity, and sickness and disease. These everyday life occurrences can have detrimental effects on the remaining years of our lives and change our existence, unless we deal with them in a healthy manner.

Broken Chains not only brings to light the detrimental effects of five life-changing tragedies, but it also shares how anyone who experiences them can be healed and delivered from their effects.

If you have experienced death of a loved one, sexual abuse, a broken relationship, the effects of promiscuity, and/or sickness and disease and have not been able to rid yourself of the emotions attached to them or specific resulting behaviors, Broken Chains is for you.

God designed each of us for a purpose, and He has an intended end for us to achieve. In order for us to effectively achieve our God-given purpose, we must be free of chains that bind us. It is not God's desire that we become immobilized by life's events. His desire is for us to be healed, delivered and set free. Be healed today, in the name of the Lord Jesus Christ!

I Have Fallen

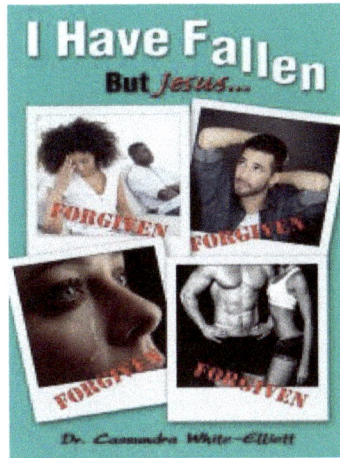

Do you know anyone who has committed his/her life to Christ but has done something unseemly that you would never expect a Christian to do? How did you feel about that person or what the person did? Did you pass judgment? What if that person were you? How would you feel if you made a misstep and no one forgave you and instead began to treat you differently? How do you feel when you are judged for past mistakes or lifestyles that are no longer part of your life?

This book shares four true stories of Christians who have made missteps during their walk with God. The purpose is not to air their dirty laundry, but to demonstrate our humanness and our vulnerability. None of us are exempt from making errors and falling into sin. It can happen to any of us.

The solution for these dilemmas is for the person who fell into sin to make a life-changing move and turn away from the sin, repent and ask God for forgiveness. His arms are waiting!

The next solution is for those who witness the sin or know of it. Pray and be of comfort to the one who has fallen. Lead him/her back to the path of righteousness. Love thy neighbor and treat him/her as you want to be treated!

The Bottom Line

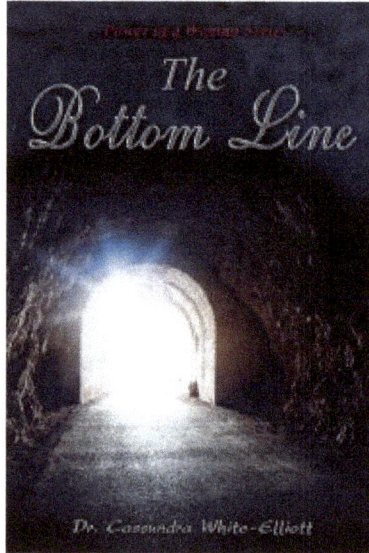

The Bottom Line is a detailed review of the Book of Job. Much can be said about Job's experiences with the loss of his children and wealth and the subsequent return of it all in mass proportions. However, the telling of Job's story in the Holy writ was not intended to focus on the return of his wealth. Instead, the focal point should be on the bottom line of the entire situation.

When you experience trials or tragedies in your life, do you tend to focus on the trial itself, the result, or the bottom line?

"What is the bottom line?" you may ask. The bottom line is the message God is sending regarding the situation.

When Job experienced his tragedies, there was a bottom line. Likewise, when you experience your trials and tragedies, there is a bottom line as well. It is up to you to discover it.

This book will reveal the bottom line in the Book of Job. It is readily apparent, but many often overlook it.

Now, it is up to you to uncover the bottom line of your experiences, for God will not bring a trial to you without a good reason.

Power of a Woman

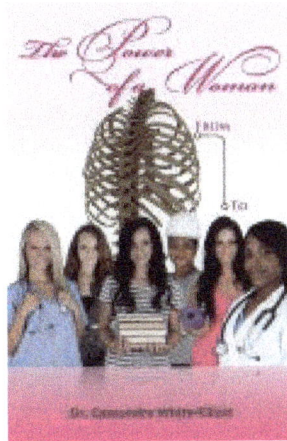

The ongoing conversation about the value of a woman is presented from a different perspective in The Power of a Woman. Dr. Cassundra White-Elliott presents a biblical perspective of women and compares it to the worldview of both yesterday and today. This comparison seeks to illustrate God's intended purpose for His uniquely designed creation: woman. Dr. Elliott shares God's truth about pre-imposed limitations set by man versus the limitations God Himself set for woman in addition to the wealth of liberality He gave her.

Women's creativity and abilities are not meant to be stifled. They are meant to be utilized to bring glory to God, to help sustain and nurture their families, and to move the world forward. Knowing God's truth will show women how to celebrate and appreciate who they are as well as one another!

Women, let's take the blinders off, lift our heads up, and march forward, side by side with men, and bring glory and honor to God! Take your rightful place with a gentle smile and grace and be who God called you to be!

Set Free

If you possess habits and display characteristics that are unbecoming, debilitating, and hinder the desired progress in your life or that affect your relationships with others, Set Free will provide the steps you need to be healed and delivered, through the Word of God.

Deliverance is available to you! Claim your healing today and walk in victory!

Do You Know God?

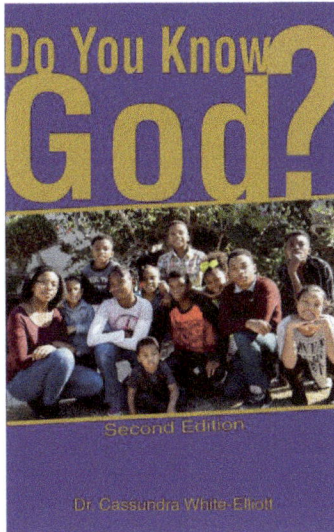

Have you or someone you know ever felt alone, confused, or unsure about your walk with God or are you unsure of what being a Christian is all about? *Do You Know God?* is an excellent text for providing answers to many of your questions. This book introduces adolescents and young adults to God in addition to answer many of their questions about being a Christian. This book shares the testimonies of the trials and tribulations that other teens have experienced and how God prevailed in their lives. All the information that is shared on the pages of the book is based upon the Word of God and the scriptures are taken from the King James Version of the Bible. If you are interested in knowing more about God's Word or how to begin your Christian experience, this book is for you.

Daughter,
God Loves You!

"... for her price is far above rubies"
(Proverbs 31:10b)

Dr. Cassundra White–Elliott

Maybe you have heard the proclamation, "The world is going to hell in a hand basket!" Well, I believe I must concur.

However, I do *not* believe, we- the adult, mature believers- should sit idly by and allow our daughters (and our sons for that matter) to go with it! We must fight for our girls and young women, for they are the mothers of tomorrow, and some may even be young mothers today. Not only will they continue the human race, but also they can have bright futures in their careers and as leaders in our society, as they allow God to direct their paths and order their steps.

Daughter, God Loves You! is an earnest attempt to address many of the issues that plague our society and turn our daughters' heads away from God.

In this book, we dive head first into topics such as God's love, the importance and impact of education, the effects of social media, overcoming abuse, and the proper perspective of the future.

For the young adult women- Reading this book will empower you to have a bright prosperous future from being enlightened about the dangers that plague our society and how to avoid pitfalls, as you walk along the path God has paved for you.

I invite all of you to take this journey with me to save our daughters and yourselves (young women) from corruption, by being empowered with knowledge.

We must thwart the plan of the enemy. So, LET'S GO!

CLF Publishing, LLC.
www.clfpublishing.org

ISBN 978-0-9961971-9-9
90000

9 780996 197199

Dr. C. White-Elliott's books are available at:
www.creativemindsbookstore.com
www.amazon.com
www.barnesandnoble.com

A Mother's Heart II

Edited by Dr. Cassundra White-Elliott

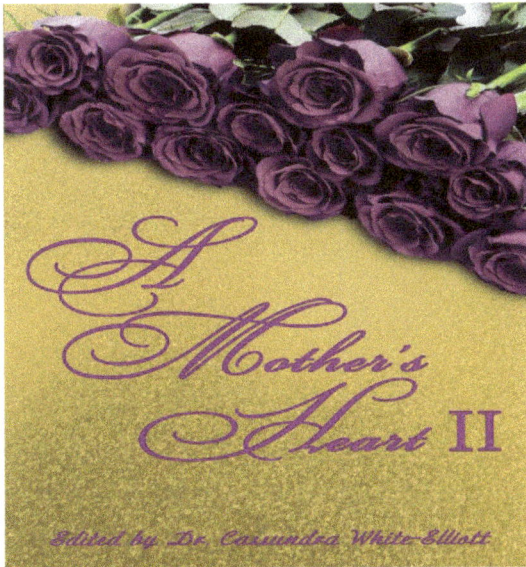

A Mother's Heart II shares the unconditional love of mothers through a compilation of testimonies. Each testimony serves as a tribute to a special mother. The children of the represented mothers have lovingly written about their childhood, young adult life and/or older adult experiences they shared with their mother. As you read the writers' reflections, you will feel the expressions of love exude from the pages.

The purpose of this book is two-fold. First, it honors those mothers who stood by their children through the trials of life and showered them with unconditional love. Second, the book is a source of encouragement for mothers who may feel inadequate and question whether or not they are actually suited for motherhood. Our advice to mothers is, *"Be encouraged; the journey of motherhood may seem daunting at times and you may shed some tears, but your children will never forget the love you have shown them and instilled in them to share with others."*

Mothers may not be perfect, but they are definitely unmatched by any other category of person on God's green earth!

The following authors are included in this compilation:

Edwin Baltierra, Shelia Bryant-Colbert, Jean Cedeno, Ilse Guadalupe Hernandez, Haley Keil, Haley King, Johnathon Lopez, Ronnette Moore, Allyson Marie Sanders, Lucas van den Elzen, Daron C. White, Ashton Wilson, Jessica Yslas, and Vanessa Zavala

CLF Publishing, LLC.
www.clfpublishing.org

Dr. Cassundra White-Elliott's books are available at:
www.creativemindsbookstore.com
www.amazon.com
www.barnesandnoble.com

ISBN 978-1-945102-02-8
90000

9 781945 102028